LESSUDDEN HOUSE, SIR WALTER SCOTT AND THE SCOTTS OF RAEBURN

Lessudden House
Sir Walter Scott
and the Scotts of Raeburn

TRESHAM LEVER

The Boydell Press · London 1971

© SIR TRESHAM LEVER 1971

FIRST PUBLISHED 1971 BY THE BOYDELL PRESS
LONDON AND IPSWICH

PRINTED IN GREAT BRITAIN BY
THE ANCHOR PRESS LTD., TIPTREE, ESSEX

ISBN 0 85 115000 4

Contents

Acknowledgements

First and foremost my thanks are due to Dr James C. Corson, formerly Deputy Librarian of the University of Edinburgh and now Honorary Librarian of Abbotsford. He placed his profound knowledge of Sir Walter Scott at my disposal, corrected my many faults, and with wonderful patience set me right on the innumerable occasions when I had taken the wrong turning. Indeed, it is not too much to say that, but for his help, this book could not have been written.

Others to whom I am grateful for help and encouragement are Mrs Patricia Maxwell-Scott and Miss Jean Maxwell-Scott, Sir Walter Scott's great great great grand-daughters who are his representatives at nearby Abbotsford; the authorities at the National Library of Scotland, Edinburgh, and especially Dr William Beattie, the former Librarian, and Mr Alan Bell, Mr Thomas I. Rae, and Miss Elspeth Yeo, all of the Department of Manuscripts; the authorities at the Scottish Record Office, Edinburgh, and especially Mr John Imrie; Miss Carola Oman, Mr W. Schomberg Scott and Mr Christopher Scott of Gala, all of whom read large parts of my typescript and offered many suggestions to correct and improve it; the Hon. Francis Hepburne-Scott, who inherited the Lessudden property from Miss Louisa Scott, the last of the Raeburn Scotts; Mr Francis Stewart, ws, who helped me over a number of difficult questions of local government in Roxburghshire and Selkirkshire at the time of Sir Walter Scott, and my Secretary, Mrs C. S. Byers.

The portraits of Walter Scott of Raeburn and his wife, the originals of which are at Abbotsford, are reproduced by kind permission of Mrs Patricia and Miss Jean Maxwell-Scott, and the photographs of Lessudden House by kind permission of the Editor of *Scottish Field*.

Preface

This is the story of a house and of the family that owned it for just over three centuries. It also tells the story of their relationship with their kinsman Sir Walter Scott, the most illustrious member of the great house of Scott.

The original Lessudden House was destroyed in the border troubles of 1544 and 1545, and the present house—much altered and embellished over the years—was built to replace it towards the end of the sixteenth century. The property was acquired about 1664 by the first of the Scotts of Raeburn, and was in their possession until the year 1968. The Scotts of Raeburn, a cadet branch of the Scotts of Harden (of which Lord Polwarth is the head), would have been of small consequence but for the fact that Sir Walter Scott was of their number. In Sir Walter's time, the laird at Lessudden was first his uncle Walter and then his cousin William, and great were the efforts that he made to forward the interests of the unfortunate and somewhat feckless Willie.

On the death in her hundredth year of Miss Louisa Scott of Raeburn, the last of her line, in 1968, the property passed to her kinsman, the Hon. Francis Hepburne-Scott, brother of Lord Polwarth. From him it was acquired by the author and his wife who, with the aid of the distinguished Edinburgh architect Mr W. Schomberg Scott, restored and beautified the house, and now make it their much loved home.

T.L.

Lessudden,
St Boswells
October, 1970

The Scotts of Raeburn

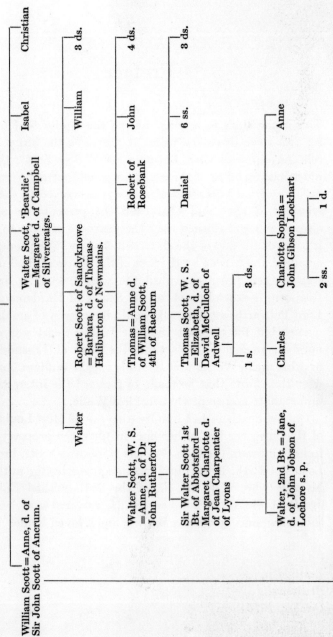

Walter Scott, 3d s. of 1st Sir William Scott of Harden
= Anne Isabel, d. of William MakDougall of Makerstoun.

William Scott = Anne, d. of
Sir John Scott of Ancrum.

Walter Scott, 'Beardie',
= Margaret d. of Campbell
of Silvercraigs.

Isabel   Christian

Walter

Robert Scott of Sandyknowe
= Barbara, d. of Thomas
Haliburton of Newmains.

William   3 ds.

Walter Scott, W. S.
= Anne, d. of Dr
John Rutherford

Thomas = Anne d.
of William Scott,
4th of Raeburn

Robert of
Rosebank

John   4 ds.

Sir Walter Scott 1st
Bt. of Abbotsford =
Margaret Charlotte d.
of Jean Charpentier
of Lyons

Thomas Scott, W. S.
= Elizabeth, d. of
David McCulloch of
Ardwell

Daniel

6 ss.   3 ds.

1 s.   3 ds.

Walter, 2nd Bt. = Jane,
d. of John Jobson of
Lochore s. p.

Charles

Charlotte Sophia =
John Gibson Lockhart

Anne

2 ss.   1 d.

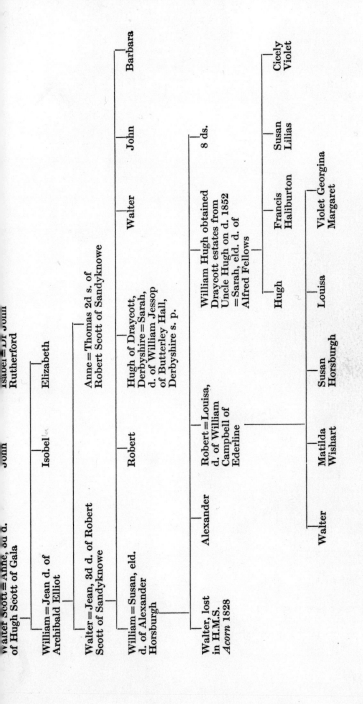

Walter Scott = Anne, 3d d. of Hugh Scott of Gala   Isobel = Dr John Rutherford

John

William = Jean d. of Archibald Elliot | Isobel | Elizabeth | Walter = Jean, 3d d. of Robert Scott of Sandyknowe | Anne = Thomas 2d s. of Robert Scott of Sandyknowe | John | Barbara

William = Susan, eld. d. of Alexander Horsburgh | Robert | Hugh of Draycott, Derbyshire = Sarah, d. of William Jessop of Butterley Hall, Derbyshire s. p. | Walter

Walter, lost in H.M.S. *Acorn* 1828 | Alexander | Robert = Louisa, d. of William Campbell of Ederline | William Hugh obtained Draycott estates from Uncle Hugh on d. 1852 = Sarah, eld. d. of Alfred Fellows | 8 ds.

Walter | Matilda Wishart | Susan Horsburgh | Louisa | Hugh | Francis Haliburton | Susan Lilias | Cicely Violet

Violet Georgina Margaret

I
LESSUDDEN HOUSE AND THE
SCOTTS OF RAEBURN

CHAPTER ONE

Years of Turmoil

Lᴇssᴜᴅᴅᴇɴ—Lessedewyne until the beginning of the sixteenth century, Lessuddene until the seventeenth— was the old name for St Boswells as well as for the house that stands at the eastern extremity of the village. The meaning is not certain but, as Leys is a court, hall, manor or fortified house, it was perhaps the home of one Edwin, of whom all trace is lost. Alternatively, as one authority suggests, it may have been derived from the Gaelic *leas aodann*, 'garden slope' or 'face';[1] and as the garden at Lessudden is on a slope that seems quite a probable explanation. The name St Boswells was not in general use before the seventeenth century, though a village with that name existed at an earlier period three-quarters of a mile south-east of Lessudden, and in that village was a church or chapel dedicated to St Boisil, prior of the monastery of Melrose. After the saintly Boisil's death from the plague in 664[2] he was succeeded by Abbot William who is said to have been obliged to check the enthusiasm of pilgrims who came to the holy man's grave in quest of miracles to the disturbance of the abbey peace. In 1170 the abbey was granted to the monks of Dryburgh, the grant being confirmed by King David's grandson, King William the Lyon (1143–1214) five years later. Unfortunately the new abbey of Melrose lay in the direct path of invasion from the south with dire consequences for its future. When the English armies sacked an abbey it was not merely for plunder but as part of a 'scorched earth' policy intended to bring starvation and bloodshed throughout the land. In the promotion of this vindictive and inhuman warfare the abbeys and their monks were fair game, and because of its position Melrose was particularly vulnerable.[3] It was first sacked in 1322 by the troops under Edward II who slaughtered the prior, William De Peebles, and murdered or seriously wounded several other monks, cast down the Host from the high altar, and stole the silver pyx. Restored in 1326 by Robert Bruce, who bequeathed his heart to it, the abbey was burnt and utterly destroyed by Richard II in the summer of 1385. In 1389 in compensation for this destruction the king granted to the convent a restriction in custom upon each 'saak' of Scottish wool, up to one thousand sacks, sent by it to Berwick-on-Tweed.

Work of rebuilding was started before the fourteenth century was out and continued with many interruptions until the early sixteenth century. Thus, as we shall in due course see, the most modern part of what remains of Melrose Abbey is only about half a century older than the present Lessudden House—or Place, as it was frequently called in days gone by.

But long before the erection of this house, a building stood on the same site. It is cause for infinite regret that little can be ascertained of the original house, save that it was L-shaped with a stair-turret, which can still be seen, projecting from the north-west wall of the main block. But if little is known of the birth and life of the ancient house, something is known of its fate.

For centuries there had been strife—bitter and merciless—on the border that divided the Kingdom of England from its northern neighbour. At first the larger kingdom had thought to crush its opponent as she had asserted her harsh supremacy over the Welsh. But Bannockburn had taught the English that the lowland Scots—Teutons, like the Saxons—were a people who might be exterminated but could not be subdued. The first of the Tudors had the wisdom to recognise these facts, and Henry VII strove hard for a reconciliation with his

turbulent neighbour. But the evils done by the Edwards
lived after them: the Scots remained suspicious and hostile,
and bloody feuds and licensed marauding continued across
the border. The farms and houses of Roxburgh—including the
Lessudden House of that day—like the farms and houses of
Northumberland were fortified by their owners who slept with
their swords beside their pillows and their horses saddled in
their stalls. Meanwhile, the Scots were thankful to strengthen
their position by an alliance with France, a country with a
special appeal for them as the ancient enemy of England. It
was in this unfavourable climate that Henry VII tried to
improve his relations with Scotland.

In 1503 he made a good start by arranging a match between
his daughter Margaret and James IV of Scotland. But the
good thus achieved was speedily thrown away by the new
king, Henry VIII. He joined the Emperor Maximilian and
King Frederick of Aragon in what was called the Holy
Alliance against France; and when in 1513 war broke out
between France and England the French sovereign reminded
King James of his obligations. The Scottish king was so ill
advised as to respond to these blandishments by invading
Northumberland with an inadequate force. He was met by an
English army under Thomas Howard, Earl of Surrey (created
in the following year Duke of Norfolk), the ablest English
general of the day, and on September 9, 1513 at Flodden
Field, between the rivers Tweed and Till, suffered an over-
whelming defeat. The warlike James desperately hurled
himself with his household upon the foe and close to Surrey's
banner met his bloody end. With him a great body of noble
Scots perished miserably in the fray. The English estimated
Scottish losses at between 10,000 and 12,000; their own at
1,500 or less. Scotland was prostrate, King Henry could have
accomplished anything; yet, wise statesman that he was, he
preferred to win the friendship of the fallen Scots by forbear-
ance rather than to press his advantage by force. The late
king of Scotland had left two sons, one aged two, the other a
posthumous infant. Therefore, a regency was necessary, and

the children's mother, Margaret Tudor, was duly voted to that office for the period of her widowhood. All might then have gone smoothly but for the unworthy behaviour of the newly appointed regent, who proved herself to be a credit neither to her country nor to her house.

We need not follow the activities of this tiresome woman or entangle ourselves in the intrigues of Angus, Albany and their followers; but it was amidst these unpromising events that King Henry VIII made his great effort at reconciliation. He proposed that his daughter Princess Mary should be betrothed to his nephew, the new Scottish sovereign, a boy of about sixteen, whose virtues were thought to be already showing themselves, whilst his vices were of later growth. Had the offer been accepted and the cousins married, future relations between England and Scotland might have been happier. Unfortunately the French influence at court was far too strong to allow this and the Estates arrogantly defied Henry to do his worst. In spite of all provocation the English king would not be put off from trying to make his nephew see reason, and when James looked like succumbing to papal intrigues that aimed at forming a coalition of Catholic princes against England, his uncle despatched Sir Ralph Sadler, a skilled diplomatist, to Edinburgh to warn his recalcitrant nephew that he was playing with fire, and to beg him to receive his uncle's overtures in the same spirit in which they were made. Had the Scottish king been free, he might have listened to this advice; but unfortunately he was under the influence of two bad counsellors, his wife Mary of Guise and David Beaton, Cardinal Archbishop of St Andrews. The whole object of this gifted man was to forge more strongly the fetters that bound Scotland to France, and to make sure that James V rejected all his uncle Henry's proposals. The cardinal was fatally successful, and as a result of his activities King Henry, though he declined ever to give up hope, never managed to come to terms with the young Scottish sovereign.

When James had been finally broken by the tragedy and the shame of Solway Moss, Beaton produced a will appointing

himself and three Scottish earls joint regents. The opponents
of the cardinal rejected this as a forgery and the Estates
declared the Earl of Arran, one of those appointed joint
regent under the will, to be Protector and Governor of the
realm. Beaton was arrested; but, as he was given into the
custody of his devoted partisan Lord Seaton, his imprisonment
was nominal and he was soon granted his freedom. Indeed,
some declared that his arrest was mainly to protect him from
the risk of being kidnapped by the English, and there may have
been something in that rather improbable story. Arran promptly concluded two treaties with England: one arranged the
marriage of the young Queen of Scots with King Henry's son,
Edward; the other concluded an alliance with England. But
no sooner was Cardinal Beaton set at liberty than he rallied
his supporters in powerful opposition both to the marriage
and to the treaty.

Arran lost his nerve. On September 3rd he rode out from
Edinburgh with three or four attendants only and, professing
anxiety for his wife's confinement at the Black Ness on
the Forth, went to join her. The next day, however, he left
for Lord Livingstone's house between Linlithgow and Stirling,
where he was met and welcomed by Beaton and Murray. They
all proceeded to Stirling, sending back messages to Linlithgow
countermanding musters on behalf of the governor. A few
days later, on Sunday September 9th, the young queen was
crowned at Stirling in the presence of them all. On September 24th, the treaties were repudiated, and on December
3rd the Scottish Parliament accepted the French offer of
alliance.

Henry VIII's prompt reply was a declaration of war.

The English sovereign was resolved on sending a force
immediately to invade Scotland with three objects in view:
first, to forward his son's marriage with Mary; secondly, to
seize Cardinal Beaton and raze his castle at St Andrews; and

thirdly, by bringing fire and sword to the borders to teach the Scots a lesson that they would never forget. In two of these objects he failed. His 'rough wooing' did not appeal to the Scots, and the wily Beaton had for long been fortifying his stronghold so that it was well-nigh impregnable except to an entrance by stealth. It was just that exception that two years later brought him to his doom. In his third object the king was horribly successful.

The commander of the force to invade Scotland was the Earl of Hertford, whose sister, Jane Seymour, Henry had married in 1536 and who had remained on excellent terms with his brother-in-law after Jane's lamented death giving birth to the future Edward VI in the following year. Hertford was a gifted commander and he had two highly competent soldiers to support him, the young Lord Shrewsbury, who was later to marry the redoubtable Bess of Hardwick, and Lord Lisle, who as Duke of Northumberland was one day to bring Hertford, by that time Lord Protector and Duke of Somerset, to an untimely end on Tower Hill. Hertford was commanded to deface Edinburgh so as to leave behind 'a fearful monument to the divine vengeance of falsehood and treachery'. He was to sack the castle, put men, women and children to the sword, and thence go to Leith and St Andrews and so punish the latter that 'the upper stone may be the nether and not one stick stand by another . . .'[4]

The invading force, assembled at Newcastle, was delayed for some days by unfavourable winds. At length the winds changed and on May 1st the whole fleet, said to be some two hundred ships, sailed from the harbour of Tynemouth, and some three days later reached the Firth of Forth.* Here they destroyed a small town to the north and seized some large boats which were to prove useful for landing. That night they anchored under the island of Inchkeith in the firth some three

---

* The account of the expedition is taken mainly from an eye-witness report sent to Lord Russell, Lord Privy Seal, by a friend of his with the army. It was probably not impartial.

miles north from the harbour of Leith. The next day, May 4th, at 9 a.m., the army landed at Granton, two miles west of Leith town, taking but four hours for completion of the operation, and they marched unopposed towards Leith. Here they were met by a Scottish force of between 5,000 and 6,000 horse and a body of foot and with them the hated Cardinal Beaton himself. However, after half an hour's fighting, when the Scots perceived that the English meant business 'and realised our devotion to see his holiness to be such as we were ready to wet our feet for that purpose, and to pass a ford which was between us and them . . . they made a sudden retreat; and leaving their artillery behind them, fled towards Edinburgh'. And of course the first man who fled was none other than 'the holy Cardinal like a valiant champion' with other leaders and great men of the realm, including the governor. Then the invaders, after repelling a determined defence of the town, took Leith, captured booty to the value of some £10,000, and seized a number of Scottish ships at anchor in the harbour, notably the *Salamander* given by the king of France at his daughter's marriage, and the *Unicorn* built by the late King James V. Indeed, they were gratified to find Leith to be 'more full of riches than we thought to have found any Scottish town to have been'. What a town it would be to keep and to fortify. How sorely Hertford regretted his instructions.[5]

The next day they marched on Edinburgh. The provost offered the keys on condition that the inhabitants be allowed to go out with bag and baggage and the city be saved from fire. The answer was a stern command for unconditional surrender. That being indignantly refused, the invaders blew in the Canongate and pillaged the capital. For two days more these troops, reinforced by some four thousand highly armed horsemen from Berwick, burnt and looted. The abbey and palace of Holyrood were set aflame; and it was the proud boast of the unknown reporter that neither within the city walls nor in the suburbs was a single house left unburnt. On May 14th they returned to Leith, smashed up and burnt the harbour pier, and so started their way homewards. 'And to give them [the Scots] better occasion to show themselves in the field against us; we left neither pile, village, town nor house in our way homewards unburnt.' Every building in Leith was destroyed. On the way back they had especial pleasure in destroying Seaton Castle because (so it was said) the owner, Lord Seaton, had assisted the hated cardinal to escape from prison.

They were also particularly enthusiastic that same day about burning 'the fair town' of Haddington, belonging to Lord Bothwell, together with its great nunnery and house of friars. But they reserved for Dunbar their greatest atrocity. They refrained from doing damage to the town by night when the Scottish force was awaiting the expected flames: but the next morning after the defenders, weary from watching and thinking the peril passed, had taken to their beds, then and then only did the invaders light their torches so that the Scots in their first sleep were encircled by a wall of fire, and men, women and children alike were suffocated in the flames.

That night the English encamped at 'a pile called Ranton', eight miles north of the border. The next day, May 18th, after destroying Ranton, the army at last entered Berwick, which they 'razed and threw down to the ground'. The whole enterprise, we are told, had cost them scarcely forty men.

So Lord Hertford returned to England in June, leaving the army in charge of Sir Ralph Evers* and Sir Brian Latoun to commit the most shameful ravages upon the Scottish border. They sacked Jedburgh, burnt the abbey, the Grey Friars and many local fortified houses. Like wild beasts they toured the border counties carrying fire and sword wherever they went, so that five months later on November 17th, according to Evers' bloody ledger, the sum total of their depredations stood thus:

---

* Evers, Evrie, Evre, Ewrie: the name is variously spelt.

Towns, towers, barnekynes, paryshe churches, bastell
houses, burned and destroyed　　　**192**
Scots slain　　　**403**
Prisoners taken　　　**816**
Nolt*　　　**10,386**
Shepe　　　**12,492**
Nags and geldings　　　**1,296**
Gayt**　　　**900**
Bolls of Corn†　　　**850**
Insight gear, etc.†† an incalculable quantity[6]

In the general destruction Lessudden was not spared. 'The
Mydle Marches', reported the just ennobled Lord Evers,§
'burnt 3 Towns called, Lussedon, longing to the Lord James;
Maxton, longing to David Litleton; Langnewton longing to the
Lord of Gradon; and toke up the same 140 Nolt with much
Insight, 24 Naggs, and in Lussedon burnt 16 strong bastele

---

* Cattle.
** Goat.
† 'A measure of capacity for grain etc. used in Scotland and the
North of England, containing in Scotland generally 6 imperial
bushels, but in the north of England varying locally from the
"old boll" of 6 bushels to the "new boll" of 2 bushels. Also a
measure of weight, containing for flour 10 stone (=140 pounds)'
OED.
†† Furniture, household goods.
§ Evers was created a peer by Henry VIII in 1544 as a reward for
the vigour with which he prosecuted the border warfare.

> *With our queen's brother he hath been,*
> *And rode rough shod through Scotland of late;*
> *They have burned the Mers and Teviotdale,*
> *And knocked full loud at Edinburgh gate.*
>
> *Now the King hath sent him a broad letter,*
> *A Lord of Parliament to be:*
> *It were well if every nobleman*
> *Stood like Lord Ewrie in his degree.*

The queen's brother was the Earl of Hertford, afterwards Duke
of Somerset, brother of Queen Jane Seymour. The 'broad letter'
was his patent of nobility. *Lord Ewrie,* Scott, *Minstrelsy* I, 363–7.

Houses, and sundry that held the same slayn, and a grete quantitie of threshed Corne and many Stacks of Corn burnt, sundry Prisonners taken, and among others Davyd Litleton's Son and Heyre, and brought away 1 Prisonner.' And from the laird Ferneyhurst's letters we learn: 'Scottishmen and Englishmen together have burnt Old Mylrose, overun Buckleugh, burnt Langnewton, run to Bewllye, Belsys and Raplaw and burnt Maxton, Saint Boylles and Lessedon . . .'[7] The next year worse was to follow. Evers and Latoun returned to Scotland at the head of an army consisting of three thousand mercenaries, one thousand five hundred Northumbrians, and a fifth column of some seven hundred discontented men, many of them prisoners taken by the English in the bloody rout in the marshes of Solway Moss, whom King Henry had used to form the nucleus of an English party in Scotland.[8] In this incursion they were if possible even more ruthless than in the previous year. Evers set fire to the Tower of Broomhouse with its aged mistress and whole family within. He again penetrated to Melrose, practically destroyed on his last visit, and pillaged what was left of abbey and of town. The marauding troops wrought havoc wherever they went, and amidst the wholesale destruction of September 1545, Lessudden was among the places 'brent, raced and cast down'.[9] The havoc was appalling.

But nemesis was coming to Evers and his followers. He did not long survive the destruction upon which he reported to his superiors with such obvious relish. As the invading army retired from the ashes of Melrose and made their way towards Jedburgh, they were shadowed by the Earl of Angus, the two-faced representative of the house of Douglas, who was lieutenant of Scotland south of the Forth, at the head of a thousand horse. On the way Angus was joined by the Master of Rothes—the warlike Norman Leslie* who a year later was to lead the party who assassinated David Beaton, the most

---

* Norman Leslie, Master of Rothes (d. 1554) eldest son of George Leslie, third or fourth Earl of Rothes, predeceased his father.

formidable, callous, and immoral of cardinals—at the head
of a body of men from Fife. The English, hesitant about
crossing the Teviot with the enemy at their heels, halted upon
Ancram Moor. Then, just as Angus was deliberating whether
to advance or retire. Sir Walter Scott of Buccleuch came up
at the head of a body of his most trusty retainers. Acting upon
the advice of this seasoned warrior, Angus retired his formidable forces from the high ground they occupied and drew
them up on a piece of low flat ground further back called
Panier-heugh or Paniel-heugh, at the same time sending a
contingent of horse to an eminence at the English rear. Lord
Evers, mistaking this cavalry for the main body of Scots in
full retreat, rushed his forces up the hill which the enemy had
just abandoned. The consternation of the English may be well
imagined when on reaching the summit they found before
them a solid phalanx of Scottish spearmen drawn up in battle
array on the flat ground below. As the Scots turned savagely
on their foes a heron, flushed from the marshes by the din of
battle, soared into the air between the opposing troops. 'Oh,'
exclaimed Angus, 'that I had here my white goss-hawk,
that we might all yoke at once!' The English, weary from their
rapid uphill march, with the sun and the wind in their faces,
were unequal to withstanding the desperate charge of the
Scottish lances. They wavered, they turned, they fled. The
pursuers, encouraging one another with the cry 'Remember
Broomhouse', slaughtered the fugitives with merciless
severity. In the fray fell Lord Evers and his son, together with
Sir Brian Latoun and some eight hundred Englishmen. A
thousand prisoners were taken. 'My lord Warden of the Middle
March and my brother are both slain together and all my
brother's men taken or slain with him; so that we are under
12 persons here that we may trust', wrote Sir Brian Latoun's
brother, Cuthbert, sadly. 'Most men of reputation are either
taken or slain, and we lack more than 20 of "his" household
servants. We might as well have been slain ourselves, for
our great friend is gone. From your castle of Norraham, the
last of Feb. at 2 a.m.'[10]

The Ancram Moor is red with gore,
 For many a southron fell;
And Buccleuch has charged us evermore
 *To watch our beacons well.**

---

* Scott, *The Eve of St John*. The ballad was composed at Mertoun, the house of Scott's kinsman, Scott of Harden, in the autumn of 1799. 'Some dilapidations had taken place in the tower of Smailholm, and Harden, being informed of the fact, and entreated with needless earnestness by his kinsman to arrest the hand of the spoiler, requested playfully a ballad, of which Smailholm should be the scene, as the price of his assent.' Lockhart, *Scott*, I, 304. In spite of the disgraceful part played by Evers in plundering Melrose and desecrating the Douglas tombs, he was buried within the abbey precincts. No resting place for his bones could be less appropriate.

CHAPTER TWO

The Scotts of Harden

IT IS not known for how long Lessudden House was left in ruins after the attacks of 1544 and 1545; but there is evidence of a building as early as 1548–9,[1] and certainly before the end of the century the new house was completed.

In the mid-sixteenth century the Scottish monasteries almost without exception were in the hands of laymen who had secured the title of abbot or 'commendator'* merely to divert the income from the monastic lands into their own pockets. James V was a grave offender in this respect. So far as is known he had seven bastards each by a different mother, for the king's taste in women was eclectic. Three of these illegitimate infants, all boys, he appointed to be abbots of Kelso and Melrose, priors of St Andrews and Pittenweem, and abbot of Holyrood respectively; a fourth was later made prior of Coldingham and a fifth abbot of the Charterhouse at Perth. Thus did the king provide for his bastards at the expense of the Church. In these early days the abbot of Melrose had a prescriptive right to the ownership of Lessudden, so James Stewart, the eldest of these infants, having been appointed Melrose Abbey's ruler, enjoyed the amenities of the property. This James** was son of Elizabeth Shaw of Sauchie. He retained his appointments and thus enjoyed his ownership of the Lessudden property for the rest of his life.

---

* One who holds a benefice *in commendam*.
** Not to be confused with another of the king's bastards, also James Stewart but by a different mother, who was to become famous as Earl of Moray (c. 1531–1570), and regent during the minority of his half-sister, Mary Queen of Scots.

On his death, the queen dowager, Mary of Lorraine, who four years previously had been made regent, appointed her brother Cardinal Guise as abbot of Melrose. But he did not enjoy his position for long; and in 1564 one Michael, who cannot be further identified, was nominated. Two years later the abbey estates, presumably including Lessudden, were granted by Queen Mary to her husband James Hepburn, Earl of Bothwell, by whose forfeiture in the following year they reverted to the Crown. In that year, 1567, following Bothwell's escape to Norway, the title of Abbot was conferred on James Douglas, second son of Sir William Douglas of Lochleven. There can be only one explanation of this strange appointment. James Douglas's mother—Lady Margaret Erskine, daughter of the fifth Earl of Mar—had been one of the many mistresses of King James V, by whom she had become mother of the other James Stewart, bastard, who had recently been made regent during the minority of his half-sister, Mary Queen of Scots, and created Earl of Moray. The affection which the kind-hearted regent bore for his half-brother must account for James Douglas's elevation and, as if these favours were not sufficient, King James VI in 1591 granted to the abbot's son, Archibald Douglas, a pension for life of 'sex monkis portionis furth of the abbey of Melros, and of the superplus of the third thereof, in consideration of the guid, trew, and thankfull service done to his hieness by his weilbelovit James, of the same abbey'. Truly, the sun of fortune was shining brightly on the ancient house of Douglas of Lochleven.

Eight years later the lands and baronies of Melrose with only a few exceptions were erected into a temporal lordship in favour of one of the king's greatest friends to whom, as he afterwards believed, he owed his life—Sir John Ramsay, shortly to be created Viscount Haddington, and later Earl of Holderness. It was Ramsay who killed both the Earl of Gowrie and his brother at the time of the Gowrie conspiracy in 1600. In 1609, Alexander Ruthven had a chartered grant of nearly all the lands and baronies belonging to the Abbey of Melrose, a handsome allowance for life being settled at the same time upon James Douglas, the Commendator. Later these estates were obtained by Sir Thomas Hamilton of Priestfield, raised to the peerage in 1613 as Lord Binning and Byres and six years later Earl of Melrose. In 1627 he suppressed his title of Melrose by patent and was created instead Earl of Hadding-ton, the Ramsay peerage of Haddington having become extinct in the previous year. He died in 1637 in his seventy-fourth year. In more recent times the monastery lands became the property of Walter Scott, Earl of Buccleuch, from whom in 1664 the Lessudden property passed to his kinsman, Walter Scott the first of Raeburn.* Early in the eighteenth century the Scott family acquired by purchase the remainder of the abbey lands included in the lordship of Melrose.

The Scotts of Harden—like those of Raeburn—are one of the many branches of the great border clan and probably the most important after the Earl of Buccleuch.** They are represented today by Lord Polwarth whose seat is Harden House near Hawick, the property of his family since 1501. But during the late sixteenth and early seventeenth century

---

* In a memorandum about Lessudden drawn up by William Scott the sixth of Raeburn in 1838 he says that the land on which the present house was built seems to have belonged in 1500 to a family of the name of Sinclair and was acquired early in 1608 by the Plummers of Middlestead from whom the first Raeburn bought it (NLS MS 3842). I do not know what authority he had for this statement which certainly does not seem to be correct.

** The pedigree goes roughly thus: In 1118 there was Uchtred Fitz-Scott, whose family continued for six generations, when there was Sir Michael Scott who fell at the Battle of Durham in 1346. His second son, John, was the first Scott of Sinton (a property near Ashkirk). The Scotts of Sinton continued for eight generations when Robert Scott, murdered in 1509, had three sons, the second of whom became called William of Harden. I am grateful to Mr Christopher Scott of Gala for this information.

they were represented by a notorious and formidable free-booter, Walter Scott, generally known as 'Auld Wat of Harden'. In his day Harden was a fortress overlooking a deep ravine of the Harden Burn; the earliest date of the present house is 1671. Auld Wat's grandfather, William, first laird of Harden, the second son of Robert Scott of Stirches, acquired the estate between 1550 and 1559 from Alexander Lord Home,[2] as well as other lands which he inherited from his brother in 1535. He had a son Walter of whom little is known save that he died in 1563 to be succeeded by his eldest son Walter. This Walter—Auld Wat—married Mary, daughter of John Scott* of Dryhope in Yarrow,[3] known for her great beauty as the Flower of Yarrow. By the marriage contract Scott of Dryhope bound himself to keep his son-in-law in meat and horse-meat at his tower of Dryhope for a year and a day. Harden for his part pledged himself to give to his father-in-law the whole of the takings from his first raid under the Michaelmas moon: he further promised that at the expiry of the period he would remove himself and his wife from Dryhope Tower without attempting to remain there by force. The bond was signed by a notary public on behalf of all the parties to it, not one of whom could sign his name. By the Flower of Yarrow Harden had ten children, six daughters and four sons.** Of the sons, two may be briefly dismissed: Hugh, who married in 1621 Jean, daughter of Sir James Pringle of Galashiels, by whom he became ancestor of the Scotts of Gala, and Francis, who married in 1624 Isobel, sister of Sir Walter Scott of Whitslaid by whom he became ancestor of Corse Scott of Synton. Of the others, William and Walter, there is rather more to tell.

In July 1611, Wat's eldest son and heir William wed Agnes Murray, daughter of Sir Gideon Murray of Elibank, and it is of this marriage that the well-known story of 'muckle-

---

* Keith Scott in *Scott 1118–1923* calls him Philip.
** Keith Scott in *Scott 1118–1923* gives seven daughters and five sons.

mouthed Meg' is told. Young Willie, captured in a fray by the
followers of Sir Gideon Murray of Elibank and carried prisoner
to Elibank Castle on Tweed bank, was offered his life if he
married the plainest of Sir Gideon and Lady Murray's three
unattractive daughters who had the additional drawback of
being known as 'muckle-mouthed Meg' (though her name
was certainly Agnes). The young laird having given his
reluctant consent to the match, the anxious parents gave
their captive no time for reflection. The marriage-contract
was executed forthwith on the parchment of a drum, and the
young couple were united before the year was out. The off-
spring of the marriage were five sons and three daughters.[4]
'It is said, they were afterwards a very happy couple', wrote
Sir Walter Scott to his friend Anna Seward. 'She had a curious
hand at pickling the beef which he stole; and, marauder as he
was, he had little reason to dread being twitted by the pawky
gowk.'[5] And the Ettrick Shepherd, who told the whole story
in his ballad *The Fray of Elibank,* testified to their happy life
together.

> *So Willie took Meg to the Forest sae fair,*
> *An' they lived a most happy an' social life;*
> *The langer he kend her, he loed her the mair,*
> *For a prudent, a virtuous, and honourable wife.*

> *An muckle gude blude frae that union has flowed,*
> *An' mony a brave fellow, an' mony a brave feud;*
> *I darena just say they are a' muckle mou'd,*
> *But they rather have still a gude luck for their meat.*

So perhaps poor Agnes was neither so plain nor so 'muckle
mouthed' after all.

A few years later tragedy struck the Harden Scotts: young
Walter, second son of Wat and the Flower of Yarrow, was
killed by Simon Scott of Bonytoun and his sons in a quarrel
about fishing rights in the river Ettrick. The defence was that
Walter had shown his 'contempt and disdane' for the fishing
and that the Bonytoun Scotts had 'onlie intendit in a solir
maner to haif dishairget suche forme of contemptuous comeing

to the said complenairis boundis foresaidis'. Unfortunately, things had got out of hand and poor Walter 'is depairtit this lyff'.[6] On hearing the news of their brother's death, so the story goes, Harden's surviving sons prepared to be avenged on his slayers. But, according to tradition, the father lured them to the dungeon of his tower, bolted the door, and hasted to Edinburgh to beg of the king the lands of the Bonytoun Scotts. Successful in his mission, he returned home, released his sons and showed them the Charter he had obtained from his Majesty. 'To horse, lads, and let us take possession!' he is said to have cried, 'These lands are well worth a dead son.'

But stories and ballads of the exploits of the old freebooter are innumerable. In the summer of 1592 he aided Bothwell in his unsuccessful attempt to seize the king at Falkland Palace: in the following winter he helped him to plunder the lands of Drumelzier and Dreva on Tweedside, when it is said that they carried off four thousand sheep, two hundred cattle, forty horses and goods to the value of £2,000. Indeed, he would have agreed with Evan Dhu Maccombich's view on Donald Bean Lean not being a cattle stealer. 'Common thief!—no such thing; Donald Bean Lean never *lifted* less than a drove in his life.' 'Do you call him an uncommon thief, then?' 'No—he that steals a cow from a poor widow or a stirk from a cotter is a thief; he that lifts a drove from a Sassenach laird is a gentleman-drover . . .'[7]

Four years later he was prominent with his kinsman, Walter Scott of Buccleuch,* in the daring raid across the border to rescue from Carlisle Castle the famous mosstrooper William Armstrong—generally known as Kinmont Willie from his castle of Kinmont (or Morton), afterwards called Sark on the Sark water in Dumfriesshire. The exploit was thought to be so hazardous that the laird of Buccleuch decreed that only younger sons and brothers of the clan should be employed. But exceptions seem to have been made in the cases of the lairds of Harden and Commonside and of Sir

---

* Walter Scott, first Baron Scott of Buccleuch (1565–1611).

Gilbert Elliott of Stobbs, the husband of Auld Wat's eldest daughter, Margaret. The Scotts maintained that Willie Armstrong had been captured during a truce, and on these grounds Buccleuch demanded his release of Lord Scrope*, Warden of the West Marches of England and governor of Carlisle Castle. On receiving no satisfactory reply Buccleuch and his followers took bold action. At the head of some two hundred determined men they presented themselves before the castle on a dark tempestuous night, undermined the postern gate and, aided no doubt by treachery from within, delivered the prisoner without being detected by the guards. Then, to the amazement of Lord Scrope, Buccleuch and his men made good their escape by fording the Eden Water in full spate.

> *Buccleuch has turned to Eden Water,*
> *Even where it flow'd frae bank to brim,*
> *And he has plunged in wi' a' his band,*
> *And safely swam them thro' the stream.*

> *He turn'd him on the other side,*
> *And at Lord Scroope his glove flung he—*
> *'If ye like na my visit in merry England,*
> *In fair Scotland come visit me!'*

> *All sore astonish'd stood Lord Scroope,*
> *He stood as still as rock of stane;*
> *He scarcely dared to trew his eyes,*
> *When thro' the water they had gane.*

> *'He is either himsell a devil frae hell,*
> *Or else his mother a witch maun be;*
> *I wadna have ridden that wan water,*
> *For a' the gowd in Christentie.'* [8]

The indignant Scrope wrote the next day to Lord Burghley and to the Privy Council to report the affair:

---

* Thomas, tenth Lord Scrope of Bolton (d. 1609), had succeeded to the offices of Warden of the West Marches of England and governor of Carlisle Castle on the death of his better-known father, the ninth Baron, in 1592.

Yesternighte in the deade tyme thereof, Water Scott of Hardinge, the chiefe man aboute Buclughe accompanied with 500 horsemen* of Buclughes and Kinmontes frendes, did come armed and appointed with gavlockes and crowes of iron, handpeckes, axes and skailinge lathers, unto an owtewarde corner of the base courte of this castell, and to the posterne dore of the same—which they undermyned speedily and quietlye, and made them selves possessores of the base courte, brake into the chamber where Will of Kinmont was, caried him awaye, and in their discoverie by the watch, lefte for deade two of the watchmen, hurt a servante of myne, one of Kynmontes keperes, and were issued againe oute of the posterne before they were discried by the watche of the innerwarde, and ere resistance coulde be made. The watch, as yt shoulde seeme, by reason of the stormye night, were either on sleepe or gotten under some covert to defende them selves from the violence of the wether; by meanes whereof the Scottes atcheived theire entreprise with lesse difficultie. The wardinge place of Kinmonte, in respect of the manner of his takinge, and the assurance he had given that he woulde not breake away, I supposed to have bin of sufficient suretie, and litle looked that any durst have attempted to enforce in the tyme of peace any of her Majestys castells, and a peece of so good strength.

And he cried loudly for revenge,

for yt wilbe a dangerous example to have this attempt unpunished. Assuringe your lordship, that if her Majesty will give me leave, yt shall cost me both life and livinge rather than such an indignitie to her highness and contempt to my selfe, shalbe tollerated. In revenge whereof, I indende that some thinge shall shortly be enterprised against the chiefe actores for repaire of this faulte, if I be not countermanded by her Majesty . . .'[9]

All of which reads like the futile burblings of a weak and foolish man.

---

* This seems to have been a gross exaggeration.

L.H.—B

Yet Scrope was neither weak nor foolish. In fact both he and Buccleuch were fiery spirits in the prime of life; the latter about thirty years of age, the former perhaps a few years older though the year of his birth is not known. Jealousy seems to have been the root cause of hostility between them. Buccleuch, who on the downfall of his stepfather, Bothwell, had managed to acquire by one means or another a considerable part of the Hepburn estates together with Hermitage Castle, had only a few years previously secured the keepership of Liddisdale, an appointment which afforded him an equal status with Lord Scrope, Warden of the Western Marches, and—if Scrope's report to Lord Burghley is to be relied upon—had made him arrogant and offensive. His messages and letters, grumbled Scrope, sounded 'a note of pryde in him selfe and of his skorne towardes me'; and he told bitterly of 'his disposition to disquiet the frontier, and disturb the peace between the princes': further, he complained that the taking of Kinmont was in breach of an assurance given at a meeting the previous March; and that, though a follower of Buccleuch, Kinmont lived within the jurisdiction of the Warden of the Western Marches so that he, Scrope, was the proper official to demand restitution.[10] This last seems to have been the chief ground of Scrope's complaint, as Evers reported to Burghley in reply to an inquiry from his superior.[11]

Thus jealous of his rival's advancement and nettled no doubt at having been made to look remarkably foolish by Buccleuch and his men, the indignant Scrope continued to demand the punishment of the delinquents. But the Queen and Burghley, realising the danger of driving her unruly subjects to desperation, took a more moderate view. Buccleuch himself was in the following year, 1597, tried by a joint English and Scottish commission and sent abroad. But all that was required of most of his followers was that in a carefully-drawn-up form they should make their submission and promise good conduct for the future. This, reluctantly and only after considerable hesitation, they did at Carlisle on January 21 of that year.[12] The signature of the redoubtable

Wat of Harden does not appear on this document—which is hardly surprising if it be true that he could not write his name!

The Flower of Yarrow remained for all her life the faithful and loyal wife of her tempestuous lord. Furthermore, if a story of her can be credited, she was also a fitting help-mate for an adventurous freebooter; for, so it is said, when the larder was low she was in the habit of serving up at his table a pair of clean spurs to indicate to her lord and their sons that it was time they rode forth for fresh provisions. This is amusingly related in the jingle by the Rev. John Marriott,* entitled *The Feast of Spurs,* included by Sir Walter Scott in the last volume of *Minstrelsy of the Scottish Border.*[13]

We have no record of the Flower of Yarrow's death, but she cannot have had a long life, for in 1598 Auld Wat married again. His second wife was Margaret Edgar of Wedderlie, widow of William Spottiswoode of that ilk. By her he had one daughter, Margaret, who married first David Pringle, Younger of Galashiels, and afterwards Sir William MakDougall of Makerstoun. Both names will reappear as our tale unfolds.

The veteran freebooter was well received by King James VI from whom he obtained several charters. He lived to a considerable age, and died, it is believed, in or about 1629,[14] when he was close on seventy years of age. In his lifetime the old man must have been what is commonly termed a character: he has become a legend since. And that legend has been kept green through the years by the lays and the ballads of the greatest of his race.

> *An aged Knight, to danger steel'd,*
> *With many a moss-trooper, came on;*
> *And azure in a golden field,*

---

* Marriott (1780–1823), after having been tutor to Lord Scott, son of the fourth Duke of Buccleuch and sixth Duke of Queensberry (who died in 1808 aged ten) became rector of Church Lawford in Warwickshire. He wrote various other poems the best known of which is *Marriage is like a Devonshire Lane.* He was an intimate of Sir Walter Scott who addressed to him the second canto of *Marmion.*

The stars and crescent graced his shield,
  *Without the bend of Murdieston.**
Wide lay his lands round Oakwood tower,
And wide round haunted Castle-Ower;
High over Borthwick's mountain flood,
His wood-embosom'd mansion stood,
In the dark glen, so deep below,
The herds of plunder'd England low—
His bold retainers' daily food.
And bought with danger, blows and blood.
Marauding chief! his sole delight
The moonlight raid, the morning fight:
Not even the Flower of Yarrow's charms,
In youth, might tame his rage for arms;
And still, in age, he spurn'd at rest,
And still his brows the helmet press'd,
Albeit the blanched locks below
Were white as Dinlay's spotless snow;
  Five stately warriors drew the sword
    Before their father's band;
  A braver knight than Harden's lord
    *Ne'er belted on a brand.***

* The Harden Scotts are descended from a younger son of a laird of Buccleuch who flourished before the Murdieston estate was acquired by the marriage of one of those chieftains with the heiress in 1296. So they bear the cognisance of the Scotts upon the field; whereas those of the Buccleuch are disposed upon a bend dexter, assumed in consequence of that marriage. Scott, *The Lay of the Last Minstrel*, Note LIV.
** *The Lay of the Last Minstrel*, Canto Fourth, ix. Incidentally, Wat had only four sons, and three after the death of Walter in 1616.

CHAPTER THREE

The Scotts of Raeburn

THE eldest son of Wat and the Flower of Yarrow was knighted by King James in his father's lifetime, and about the middle of the seventeenth century he acquired the estate of Mertoun.* During the Civil War he remained faithful to the king and in 1654 paid for his loyalty with a fine of £3,000 imposed by Oliver Cromwell. Sir William Scott of Harden's third son, Walter, often called Wat Warspurs or Hotspurs, was the first Scott of Raeburn. He took the name from a Dumfriesshire estate which he farmed for some years. At that time he lived at the Old Red Tower at Dalcove, a farm between the Mertoun and Makerstoun estates the house of which has long ceased to exist. Thanks to his great-great-grandson we have some of this Walter Scott's farming memoranda, which his descendant copied out in 1848, and some extracts from these are not without interest:

> *13 May 1664.* I began to give the fauch** the sumer furze upon the 13 May 1664 and had done with it the 27 May 1664 at morning.
>
> *14 June 1664.* I began to weed the corne upon which day all the wheat was fairly shot,† and had done with weeding it upon the midle of Julie 1664.
>
> *26 Julie 1664.* I began to lead the peits†† wt. the towne hors viz. 12 stacks of Huntleywood peits and six stacks of (?) Fanns and had done with leading them upon the 13th Agust 1664.

---

* Now the home of the Duke and Duchess of Sutherland.
** Fallow.
† Grown or sprouted.
†† Cart the peat.

> *5 Agust 1664.* I began to lead out the sumer muck to the wheat. . . .
>
> *1 Ag. 1664.* Thomas haistie in Delcove fied to sheare* all harvest also to work in the barne yaird till all the corne be inned for £7 00s 00d.**

In addition Haistie was to receive a 'bonnteth'† of 'one full of beare and one half full of peis'.

> *2 Ag. 1664.* Walter Mackdugall in Mackerstoune 'fied to sheare all harvest for £007 00s 00d' and furthermore he was to receive a bonnteth of one full of beare.
>
> *2 Ag. 1664.* Isabell Mackdugall in Mackerstoune— [presumably Walter's wife or daughter] was 'to sheare all harvest for £005 00s 00d' and to receive by way of 'bonnteth' 'one full of beare'.
>
> *2 Ag. 1664.* Jennet Leck in Makerstoune fied to sheare all harvest for £005 00s 00d.

and so on with other servants. Clearly no equality of the sexes in the seventeenth century!

The weather that summer was warm, it seems, and the harvest was swiftly gathered in. 'I did begin the harvest upon the 17th Agust, 1664 being Wednesday and had done with the harvest upon the 3rd Sept. 1664.'

This was followed by details of the crop harvested at Dalcove.

In addition, in September Walter Scott was able to record that he got from John Cochrane, Tenant in Lessudden, three bolls†† of oats and from Mark Kyle in Lessudden two bolls of

---

* To reap with sickle or scythe.

** All sums in these memoranda are £s Scots, not Sterling.

† A gift stipulated for in addition to money wages. The word is known only since the fifteenth century and in later times only in Scotland. (OED).

†† A measure of capacity for grain, etc. used in Scotland and the north of England, containing in Scotland generally 6 imperial bushels, but in the north of England varying locally from the 'old boll' of 6 bushels to the 'new boll' of 2 bushels. Also a measure of weight, containing for flour 10 stone (=140 pounds) (OED.)

oats at £4 6*s.* 8*d.* the boll, 'which was bought for the hors'.[1]

It was in this very year that Raeburn acquired the property of Lessudden and it was obviously with some pride that he recorded his transactions with his tenants. This new possession standing on the opposite bank of the Tweed to Mertoun and just outside the small village of St Boswells was to become his and his descendants' principal residence for just over three centuries.

What a beautiful and romantic district for the homes of the lairds of Harden and of Raeburn; and, thanks to his son-in-law and biographer, we know how it affected the greatest and the most romantic of the clan when as a boy he used to stay with his paternal grandfather at the farm-house of Sandyknowe, near Smailholm Tower, the scene of *The Eve of St John* and described in the third Canto of *Marmion*. 'On the summit of the Crags which overhang the farm-house [Sandyknowe] stands the ruined tower of Smailholme', writes Lockhart,

and the view from thence takes in a wide expanse of the district in which, as has been truly said, every field has its battle, and every rivulet its song:

> *The lady looked in mournful mood,*
> *Looked over hill and vale,*
> *O'er Mertoun's woods, and Tweed's fair flood,*
> *And all down Teviotdale.*

Mertoun, the principal seat of the Harden family, with its noble groves; nearly in front of it, across the Tweed, Lessudden, the comparatively small but still venerable and stately abode of the Lairds of Raeburn; and the hoary Abbey of Dryburgh, surrounded with yew-trees as ancient as itself, seem to be almost below the feet of the spectator. Opposite him rise the purple peaks of Eildon, the traditional scene of Thomas the Rymer's interview with the Queen of Faerie; behind are the blasted peel which the seer of Erceldoun himself inhabited, 'the Broom of the Cowdenknowes', the pastoral valley of the Leader, and the bleak wilderness of Lammermoor. To

the eastward the desolate grandeur of Hume Castle*
breaks the horizon, as the eye travels towards the range
of the Cheviot. A few miles westward, Melrose, 'like
some tall rock with lichens grey', appears clasped amidst
the windings of the Tweed; and the distance presents the
serrated mountains of the Gala, the Ettrick, and the
Yarrow, all famous in song. Such were the objects that
had painted the earliest image on the eye of the last and
greatest of the Border Minstrels.[2]

This first Scott of Raeburn married Anne Isobel Mak-
Dougall,** daughter of William MakDougall of Makerstoun,
'a family of great antiquity and distinction in Roxburghshire',† and in 1657 husband and wife had a remarkable
experience. In that year the dynamic George Fox, founder of
the Society of Friends, travelled north of the border on one
of his missionary journeys, and (as he afterwards recorded)
'as he first set his horse's feet upon Scottish ground he felt
the Seed of Grace to sparkle about him like innumerable
sparks of fire'. Raeburn and his wife met Fox and the young
couple were so impressed by the zeal and eloquence of that
remarkable man that they then and there decided to embrace
the Quaker faith. This required courage, for it was a time
when the Society of Friends was subject to bitter persecution.
However all seems to have gone well with them for several
years, until in 1664 Anne Isobel's brother suddenly decided

---

* Hume or Home Castle in Berwickshire is a massive stone building
with exaggerated castellated battlements built by the last Earl
of Marchmont in 1794 and now owned by the Department of
Agriculture and Fisheries.
** Some confusion has been caused by the fact that she is sometimes
referred to by her first and sometimes by her second Christian
name.
† Lockhart, *Scott* I, 71. They are believed to have started about
1230 when the first MakDougall moved from Galloway and acquired
lands from the abbot of Kelso. For this information I am grateful
to Mr Christopher Scott of Gala who is a descendant of the family
as the estates of Gala and Makerstoun became amalgamated in
the last century.

to take the three children, William, Walter and Isobel,*
from their mother to be brought up at Makerstoun. The
distracted mother, so it is said, followed them from Lessudden
and, when denied entrance by the MakDougalls, she fell on
her knees before the gates of her family home and prayed
that those who had so cruelly separated mother and children
should suffer themselves by having no heir to succeed them.
Her prayer was granted: the male line of the second Sir
William of Harden became extinct in 1710, and the represen-
tation of Makerstoun soon passed into the female line.

In the following year Raeburn and Makerstoun brought
the matter before the Privy Council. This august body, having
considered the whole matter, decreed thus:

> *Edinburgh, 20 June, 1665.* The Lord of his Majesty's
> Privy Council having received information that Scott of
> Raeburn, and [Anne] Isobel Mackdougall, his wife, being
> infected with the error of Quakerism, doe endeavour to
> breid and traine up William, Walter, and Isobel Scott,
> their children, in the same profession, we therefore give
> order and command Sir William Scott of Harden, the
> said Raeburn's brother, to seperat and take away the
> saids children from the custody and society of the saids
> parents, and to cause educat and bring them up in his
> owne house, or any other convenient place, and ordaines
> letters to be direct — at the said Sir William's instance
> against Raeburn, for a maintenance to the saids children,
> and that the said Sir Wm. give ane account of his dili-
> gence with all conveniency.

And again in the following year:

> *Edinburgh, July 5, 1666.* Anent a petition be Sir Wm.
> Scott of Harden, for himself and in name and behalf of
> the three children of Walter Scott of Raeburn, his brother,
> showing that the Lords of the Council, by ane act of the
> 27th day of Junn 1665, did grant power and warrand
> to the petitioner, to seperat and take away Raeburn's

---

* There was a fourth child, Christian, born after Scott's release
from prison.

children, from his family and education, and to breed them in some convenient place, where they might be free from all infection in their younger years from the principalls of Quakerism. And, for maintenance of the saids children, did ordain letters to be direct against Raeburn; and, seeing the Petitioner, in obediance to the said order, did take away the saids children, being two sonnes and a daughter, and after some pains taken upon them in his owne family, has sent them to the city of Glasgow, to be bread at schools, and these to be principled with the knowledge of the true religion, and that it is necessary the Council determine what shall be the maintenance for which Raeburn's three children may be charged, as likewise that Raeburn himself, being now in the Tolbooth of Edinburgh, where he dayley converses with all the Quakers who are prisoners there, and others who daily resort to them, whereby he is hardened in his pernitious opinions and principills, without all hope of recovery, unless he is desparat for such pernitious company, humbly therefore desyring that the Councell might determine upon the soume of mony to be payed be Raeburn, fir the education of the children, to the petitioner, who will be countable therefor; and that, in order to his conversion, the place of his imprisonment may be changed. The Lords of his Maj. Privy Councell having at length heard and considered the foresaid petition, do modifie the soume of two thousand pounds Scots . . . and ordaines the said Walter Scott of Raeburn to be transported from the tolbooth of Edinburgh to the prison of Jedburgh, where his friends and others may have occasion to convert him . . . and where other Quakers must be forbidden to approach him.

Raeburn's imprisonment in Jedburgh jail can only have been short, for he was soon back at Lessudden, where he and Anne spent the rest of their days enlarging and beautifying their newly acquired property.

All things considered, it is not surprising that the family feud was still unabated eight years later. At the same time it is comforting to know that the unfortunate couple received

sympathy from at least one MakDougall, Raeburn's younger
brother-in-law William, who was disgusted at the malicious
conduct of both families. 'Dear brother', he wrote to Raeburn
early in 1673

> I am glad to hear by yours of my sister and your good
> health; but sorie that our brothers should continue in ther
> wonted malise and un-Christian dealings with you which
> I am confident if your business war well adressed ether
> heir by Courte or to our Counsell in Scotland you might
> not allone be freed from their malice for the dammage
> of your Estate brot to ther grate shame if they trulie
> considered the dewties of humanitie: brother I will
> forbeir the inlarging my meining in many words only
> desyring your lissence to make your case known to
> Lauderdale or someone else I sall find fitting or able to
> get you releved from the dispytifull ussage of your
> relations.

Whether or not William MakDougall really had any influence
with the all-powerful Duke of Lauderdale,* the intimate of
the king and since his restoration in 1660 Secretary for Scottish
Affairs, it is impossible to say: nor do we know what answer
Walter Scott of Raeburn returned to his kindly brother-in-
law, who thus ended his letter: 'lett me heir from you with
the first, my deer luv to my sister yourself and Christian, I
am your brother till death, Will Makdugall'.[3]

In view of all the tribulations that Walter and Anne Scott
had to bear at the hands of their families, it is perhaps
surprising that they had the heart and the inclination to
make improvements to their house. But so it was; indeed,
the great interest of their lives henceforth was the care and

---

* John Maitland, second Earl and first Duke of Lauderdale
(1616–82), eldest surviving son of John, second Lord Maitland of
Thirlestane, created first Earl of Lauderdale, and great nephew of
William Maitland of Lethington, the minister of Mary Queen of
Scots. The Duke was born at Lethington—now called Lennoxlove
and the home of the Duke and Duchess of Hamilton—and died at
Tunbridge Wells. He was buried at Haddington.

maintenance of the home they loved. Unfortunately we do not know much of the state of the rebuilt house when Raeburn took possession in 1664, except for the perhaps rather unreliable memorandum drawn up by the sixth Raeburn in his old age in 1838.[4] When his ancestor acquired the property, he tells us, the house was a 'Border strength' with small windows and 'all underparts arched', by which he presumably means the ground floor rooms in the central block were vaulted, as we know they were. A narrow staircase then led from what he calls the 'vault' by which he obviously means the vaulted room (which in his day was used as a kitchen) to the upper storeys. This staircase, where the buttresses are now, was not then visible, but ascended in the wall of the house. Lessudden in the seventeenth century was surrounded by a strong wall with a gateway to the north, and within the wall were the gardens, a large circular pigeon house and a well. In front—for the entrance front was on the south side in those days—were the stables, and to the west 'the malt-barn' and other offices. The public road, then called the Lidgate, so William Scott records, then ran past the very end of the house. He has left us a drawing of what he says the property looked like when Walter and Anne acquired it.

Be that as it may they soon set about enlarging and beautifying the property, and they commemorated their work of restoration by placing their armorial panel, which can still be seen, on the south-eastern wall above the present terrace with a shield charged for Scott of Raeburn—two mullets in chief, in base a crescent, with the crest a female figure. This once bore the date 1666 but weathering of the stone has long since obliterated the figures. In addition to this a wrought-iron knocker bearing the date 1685 and two sets of initials, W.S. and A.S. commemorate the restoration work to Lessudden undertaken by Walter and Anne Scott.* Their alterations

---

* This knocker, lost for a time, was found in a bad state of repair by the previous owner, the Hon. Francis Hepburne-Scott. He restored the knocker and generously returned it to the present owner. It is now fixed on the garden door.

included the enlargement of the windows, the redecoration of the first storey rooms, extensive embellishments to the second floor, the building of a new wing to the north-east so as to extend the size of the house; and (most noteworthy of all) the removal of the old newel staircase (the turret of which still exists) and in its place the building in the short arm of the L of the much larger and impressive scale and platt stair supported by Tuscan columns, which dates from about 1685. The first flight of this stairway and its balustrade are of stone throughout: the upper flights, otherwise identical, are of oak. It has an exact parallel, though in pine throughout, at nearby Fairnington, three and a half miles south-west of Roxburgh. It is this remarkable staircase that gives much of the charm to present-day Lessudden. 'The austere, unassuming and typically Scottish exterior, with its stepped gables and high proportions', writes Mr Mark Girouard in his article on the house in *Country Life*:

> is no preparation for what meets the eye when one enters the door. It seems as though one has wandered by mistake through one of the side doors of an Austrian or North Italian palace; for I know of nothing else in the British Isles quite like the Lessudden staircase. It is certainly, not remotely English in character; but neither is it typically Scottish, although the Scots had in the 17th century a fondness for stone (usually newel) stairs and for massive square balusters, the latter used both on staircases and, more often, as exterior decoration. But what is distinctive at Lessudden is the way a staircase of this type is entered through a screen of Tuscan columns, and it is this continuation which is so reminiscent (even if on a small scale and in a provincial idiom) of Continental late Renaissance and Baroque.[5]

According to William Scott's memorandum on the property it was the second Raeburn who removed the vaulted ceiling which then ran the whole length of the central block, the length of which he says is forty-four feet, enlarged the windows and replaced the grey slates on the roof with blue ones. Scott also records that this laird was responsible for the magnificent panelling still to be seen in two of the rooms on the first floor and in other ways ornamented and beautified his home. William Scott's father, the fifth Raeburn, removed the Court Yard shown in his diagram and the well about the year 1771 and built the present stables; whilst he himself, after becoming the sixth laird 'again repaired the House and made the Place as it now is'.[6]

Today the once vaulted room has been divided so as to form a square hall and off it a large dining-room. Through this is a small breakfast room and beyond the kitchen quarters. On ascending the remarkable stairs, already described, one comes on the first floor to a lobby leading to a small boudoir which looks over the modern front entrance. To the right is the drawing room, spacious and attractive but not architecturally impressive, to the left are the two rooms with the fine seventeenth-century panelling said to have been supplied by the second laird. Their bolection-moulded fire-places are flanked by pilasters, those in the first room (the library) being Composite, those in the second (a bedroom) Ionic. Beyond the bedroom is a bathroom. The rooms on the second floor have been much altered recently, and consist of a suite of bedroom, dressing room and bathroom, a single and a double bedroom and a bathroom. Above are a work room, attics and lumber rooms. Further accommodation is to be found in the cottage which is now joined to the house.

Walter Scott the first of Raeburn died in or about 1693 aged seventy-nine.* He left two sons, William and Walter. The elder succeeded his father as Raeburn and married Anne, daughter of Sir John Scott of Ancrum. The younger, Walter, was soon showing himself to be a person of singular character. He was a man of great courage and determination. He bore arms under John Graham of Claverhouse Viscount Dundee and the Jacobite Earl of Mar;** and after the Revolution he

---

* Keith Scott in *Scott, 1118–1923* says he died 'before 1688', on what evidence I do not know.
** John Erskine, sixth or eleventh Earl of Mar (1675–1732).

became himself a keen Jacobite. Because of his vow never to shave until the Stuarts were restored to the throne, he was known in the family as 'Beardie'. He is thus immortalised by his great grandson in verse:

> *And thus, my Christmas still I hold*
> *Where my great grandsire came of old,*
> *With amber beard, and flaxen hair,*
> *And reverend apostolic air—*
> *The feast and holy-tide to share,*
> *And mix sobriety with wine,*
> *And honest mirth with thoughts divine:*
> *Small thought was his, in after time*
> *E'er to be hitch'd into a rhyme.*
> *The simple sire could only boast,*
> *That he was loyal to his cost;*
> *The banish'd race of king revered,*
> *And lost his land,—but kept his beard.* [7]

And more soberly in prose. 'It would have been well that his zeal had stopped there', wrote Sir Walter Scott in his autobiography. 'But he took arms and intrigued in their cause, until he lost all he had in the world, and, as I have heard, ran a narrow risk of being hanged, had it not been for the interference of Anne, Duchess of Buccleuch and Monmouth',[8] the head of his family, widow of the Duke of Monmouth of unfortunate memory. Afterwards, he was forced to live in strict retirement, subsisting mainly on the fortune of his wife, a Campbell of Silvercraigs.

We have a rather delightful picture of Beardie attending the funeral of his wife's father. 'My dear', he wrote to her from Glasgow on February 2, 1714,

He was buried yesterday . . . very devoutlie and honorablie for Blythswood had ordered all things proper and suitable to a nicety. All the gentlemen in the place the Magistrates and the citizens of best esteem and substance accompanied the funeral in very good order. I carried the head, Blyswood on my right and Bell, Lizzie's husband, on my left hand, other nearest relations and

Sr. James Campbell of Auckinleck carried all the way.
After the funerall there was prepared in the large roome
of the Coffee House a very handsome and genteele treat,
to which the Magistrates and gentlemen and friends
were invited. The treat consisted of confections, sweet-
breads, and bisket of divers sorts very fine and well done,
and wines there was at it upwards of thirtie. We are
to-day to look at his papers. . . . My dear, Your Wa.
Scot. Mistress Scot in Lessudwyne to the care of Mistrs.
Meinzies [his sister] in Edr. to be forwarded.[9]

Let us hope that the daughter was satisfied with the arrangements for her father's funeral. Beardie himself died in Kelso
on November 3rd, 1729.

Beardie's elder brother and his wife, it seems, lived quietly
at Lessudden intent on bringing up their family, two boys,
Walter and John, and a girl, Isobel. This second Raeburn was
a quiet country gentleman, fond of dogs and horses and of high
living: 'no gentleman', he was wont to say, 'died of drinking
but many in learning to drink'. His younger son John lived
to become a lieutenant in Colonel Thomas Howard's Regiment
of Foot, but what subsequently became of him is not known.
His daughter Isobel married Dr John Rutherford. Of the
elder son Walter there is unfortunately more to tell.

It is indeed sad that the father did not live long enough to
control the passions of this headstrong son, who when his
father died on August 6, 1699 at the early age of forty-one,
was only sixteen years of age. It was not long before the
wayward boy was learning to live the life of a gentleman of
fashion. Thus we have the young laird's 'Accompt with
Andrew Rutherford Chirwigeon', dated May 20, 1702, which
contains such items as 'balls for horses 01 10 00'*; '3 ounces
of flower of brimston 00 12 00'; '4 ounces of anneseeds
00 04 00'; 'ane ounce of oyl of white Lillies 00 11 00'; '2

---

* 'Bolus, a medicine in the form of a ball or large pill. *1720:
London Gazette,* No. 5831/4, The Cordial Horse Balls at 41*s.* per
pound' (OED).

ounces of anodine oyl 00 09 00'; '2 ounces of anodine spirit 01 01 00'; '2 doses of purgeing pills gilded 01 10 00'; '2 purgeing potions'; 'ane ounce of purgeing syrup'; followed immediately by '3 ounces of purgeing syrup'; and so forth. What was worse, young Walter was soon beginning to show himself to be a self-willed, foul-tempered young man with a strong taste for drink. At first all seemed set fair for him. On the death of his father he became the third of Raeburn; on November 20, 1703 he married at Galashiels Anne, youngest daughter of his kinsman and neighbour, Hugh Scott of Gala, by whom he became the father of a son and two daughters, christened William, Elizabeth and Isabella. Then came tragedy.

On Friday October 3, 1707 this lucky man to whom fortune had been so bounteous came to an untimely end in a field on the outskirts of Selkirk, still known as Raeburn's Meadow.* At the age of twenty-four he was killed in a duel with Mark Pringle of Crichton, youngest son of Andrew Pringle of Clifton. Six days later, and five days after the funeral, there assembled at Lessudden House a great gathering of friends and relatives of the dead laird. Those present included Sir Patrick Scott of Ancram and Walter Scott of Raeburn (his uncles), Sir James Scott of Gala and his brother Thomas, Robert Scott of Harden, and John Hoppringle of that ilk. The assembled company considered and made careful notes of the financial position of Walter's unhappy widow and children, made provision for the three fatherless infants, and embodied their conclusions in a lengthy memorandum which

---

* Now the site of the Raeburn Meadow building estate. 'The place where the duel was fought is well known and in a Park belonging to the heirs of the late Mr Andrew Henderson and called Raeburn's Meadow. . . . The park is one containing about 5 acres, and has now no appearance of meadow in it, having been converted into arable land, but the meadow was the hollow ground near the head of the Park and the duel was fought in the middle of the hollow ground.' Andrew Lang (Sheriff Clerk of Selkirkshire) to Sir Walter Scott, Abbotsford. NLS MS 3899 f. 201.

they deposited in a cabinet at Lessudden House where it must have remained for a great many years.[10] They were careful to confine all that they minuted to matters of strict business. It is difficult to believe, however, that the gathering did not also consider the circumstances of the quarrel that had led up to the duel; but, if they did, no written record has survived. In consequence, little was known of the affair until one hundred and thirty-three years later when papers were found at the Pringles' family home, The Haining, on the outskirts of Selkirk, that gave an account of the whole unhappy story. On January 30, 1840 Alex. Pringle wrote to tell Raeburn that in opening a box of old papers that could not have been seen for fifty years and that was entirely unknown to him he had come across some details of the sad events of 1707, and that he was sending the papers to Lessudden. 'The combatants were', he added, 'in the same degree of affinity to you and myself, namely our respective great grand sire.'[11] No answer from Raeburn has been found, but in fact he wrote at least three letters, as the next from Pringle shows. 'My dear Raeburn', he wrote on November 26th the same year,

> I have three of your letters to acknowledge; but have been prevented by interruptions as well as by a wish to send you some notes on your pedigree. I . . . now return you Mark Pringle's Petition.[12] The perusal of it was a treat to me, but I agree with you though it is desirable to lay it by amongst your family papers, and only shew it to friends who are curious and interested in these things. The impression which it leaves is a painful one (though it must be borne in mind that the statement is *ex parte,* and in the circumstances necessarily as unfavourable to the one party as it is favourable to the other).
>
> All that need be said of it in a genealogy is that your unhappy ancestor was killed in a duel occasioned by a quarrel in the heat of liquor with M.P. etc. an occurrence unhappily not singular in the country at that period. I should like much to peruse your other documents on the subject, as well as your other family memorials, and

hope that I may some day get an opportunity of doing
so at Lessudden. . . .[13]

And six years later Raeburn wrote from Lessudden to tell
his kinsman, Sir William Scott of Ancram, that he had
recently seen in old family papers an account which shed an
entirely new light on the duel, unknown for over a century,
which, he added, 'The late Sir Walter Scott tried to obtain
in vain.'[14]

Now it seems highly unlikely that these papers were the
same as those which Pringle had shown to Raeburn six years
previously which after all was quite a long time ago. Furthermore, Pringle would have had no reason to deny a sight of
these papers to Sir Walter Scott, for they did no harm to the
memory of his (Pringle's) ancestor; and if he was prepared
to show them to Raeburn, why not to Sir Walter? It seems
much more likely that they were the 'other documents on the
subject' [i.e. the duel] referred to by Pringle in his letter to
Raeburn of November 26, 1840. Were they then a Raeburn
version of the affair suppressed by the family gathered in
force at Lessudden on that melancholy occasion in October,
1707? And is it correct that Sir Walter Scott was not allowed
to see them?

In October 1830 Scott wrote to his cousin Willie, who had
in May of that year succeeded his father as laird of Raeburn,
asking to see some old family papers, and his letter of request
is marked 'Sent him the old papers mentioned.'[15] From all
we know of Scott, we can be sure that he would be most
anxious to read family papers dealing with the duel, so were
not these papers perhaps a Lessudden version of the affair,
hitherto suppressed by the family because of the injury they
did to the memory of the young Raeburn who fell in the
encounter? Whether Sir Walter was able to read them we
cannot tell. He was mortally ill at the time and it was later
in the month of October that he sailed from Portsmouth for
a milder climate, a cruise from which he returned only to
die. Did he, in those few days between receiving the papers
and sailing return them to Lessudden? If, as is very probable,

he did not do so, may they even yet be one day found in some forgotten drawer or box at Abbotsford? It is an intriguing thought, for it is a misfortune that no documents from Lessudden have been found to corroborate or to amend the Pringle story, a version of what led up to the encounter very damaging to the memory of the Raeburn who fell in the fray. It is a misfortune that we have only The Haining account of what took place at that fatal meeting more than two and a half centuries ago.

CHAPTER FOUR

The Haining Version

O N THURSDAY October 2, 1707, a great assembly of
gentlemen of the shire convened by the Lord Clerk
Register, Sir James Murray of Philiphaugh, father-in-law of
John Pringle, Mark's brother, had met at the Michaelmas
Court in Selkirk. At this gathering most of the leading men
of the county were present, including (among others) Sir
Patrick Scott of Ancrum, the lairds of Wooll, Ashiesteel,
Ancrum the younger, Robert Kerr (brother of Andrew Kerr
of Chatto), and of course Walter Scott of Raeburn and Mark
Pringle, as well as the County Clerk Andrew Wauch. Whilst
the meeting lasted, nothing untoward happened and the
whole company parted in the best of humour. Thereafter
young Walter Scott went to another house in Selkirk—
presumably an inn—where Mark Pringle and a servant happened to be. It was soon evident that Scott had drunk more
than was good for him, for he fell to abusing an inoffensive
townsman of Selkirk who chanced to be present and chased
him out of the house. A little later, when two of the company
began quarrelling, Mark Pringle, it seems, played the peacemaker and with the help of others parted the contestants.
Whereupon Walter Scott without any provocation whatsoever accosted Pringle calling him damned rogue and rascal
and in a fury either offered to horse-whip or did actually lash
him. Evidence on the point is at variance. At this Pringle
mildly asked: 'Watty, what illeth you at me, for assure yourself I will not quarrel with you'; and the Laird of Torwoodlie
came up to Mark and begged him as a friend not to take
notice of what had passed. At the same time, Thomas Scott of
Gala took his brother-in-law aside and told him to his face

that he was entirely in the wrong. All the answer he received was a flourish of the horse-whip and a growl that Pringle deserved what he had got. Yet Thomas Scott hoped that Raeburn's fury might abate, especially when in presence of all the company Mark Pringle made a conciliatory gesture. 'Raeburn,' he said, 'let there be no more of it. If I have given offence to you I will beg pardon of you and them, and I hope you will do the like to them and me, if any offence is come of you.' Not only did Raeburn refuse to be pacified but he continued to insult the unfortunate Pringle with opprobrious language, to menace him with his whip and, when he could break away from the friends trying to restrain him, to whisper in Mark's ear that he demanded satisfaction the very next morning. At this the company parted. Thomas Scott, still hoping that the morrow might see the end of the affair, went to spend the night with James Murray, a friend in Selkirk; and Pringle went to his mother's house, The Haining, just outside the town.

Meanwhile Raeburn's passion did not cool, for, having taken horse and ridden furiously through the streets of Selkirk, he at length came to the entrance of Pringle's house, where one of Mrs Pringle's servants heard him exclaim in a loud voice, 'Damn him, is he gone in?' But she resolutely refused to admit him. So, balked of his prey, at between midnight and one in the morning he came to Murray's house and lay down on the bed beside his brother-in-law. At about seven they both awakened and Thomas once again reproved Walter for his monstrous conduct. 'Do not you mind how impertinent you was to Mr Pringle and the company yesternight?' he asked. 'But I hope the quarrel is over.' Vain hope: Raeburn made little or no reply until, having risen and dressed hurriedly, he said, 'I will put on your jockey coat* because it is a rainy morning'; and so saying he went downstairs. Yet in spite of this Thomas still did not fear serious trouble, until,

---

* Jockey coat: 'a form of great coat (? formerly worn by horse-dealers)' (OED).

after summoning Raeburn's servant and asking what had become of his master, he received the answer that he did not know but that he had taken a horse from the stable and was gone.

At this news Thomas Scott at last became seriously alarmed. He rose in haste, went to the next room where the laird of Ashiesteel was in bed and awakened him. He told him of Raeburn's departure and expressed the fear that he had gone to The Haining to get Mark Pringle. Whereupon the two men made for the house with all possible speed, only to be greeted before they reached the house with the grim news that both Raeburn and Pringle had gone forth.

Earlier that morning, Walter Scott, on his way on horseback to The Haining, had by chance come upon a workman going in the same direction, and requested him to enquire at the house if Mark Pringle was within. The man soon returned with the news that Pringle had left home about an hour previously. Then Scott turned his horse about and rode through the town in search of his quarry. At length he came up with him, only to be asked what he was quarrelling about. 'Don't you remember,' came the furious reply, 'that your hat touched my face, when you and the company were blowing out the burnt brandy?' There was really no answer to such imbecility and the two young men—the one blinded with fury, the other striving to make his companion see reason—rode through Selkirk town together, accompanied only by a servant. In spite of all that Pringle could say his companion would not be gainsaid. Yet he continued again and again to implore the infuriated Walter to be pacified. But Raeburn, beside himself, continued to demand satisfaction, so that at length his unfortunate companion could find no way to avoid fighting a duel over a quarrel that for him did not exist.

The encounter took place on the outskirts of Selkirk. It had not proceeded long before Scott received a slight scratch in the arm. Pringle seized this excuse once again to beg his adversary to be satisfied. But Scott savagely refused, and insisted that the fight must continue. In a very few minutes

Scott received a second wound, this time on the hand, and it caused considerable bleeding: whereupon Pringle yet again entreated him to forbear. But his pleading was in vain. His adversary, swearing an oath that they should not both leave the field alive, only fought the more violently; and, seeing that he was showing himself to be by far the less skilled swordsman, the more violently he fought the more reckless became his sword play. And so the unequal contest advanced to its fatal conclusion: a thrust from Pringle's sword penetrated deep into his adversary's right side. Seeing Scott stagger, Pringle ran towards him, laid him on the ground and expressed his sorrow that Walter's obstinacy had let the matter go so far: to which he received the churlish reply that this was not the end of the matter and that they should renew their trial on another occasion.

But it was the end of the matter. Scott's friends carried him into the town of Selkirk, where, after having been blooded, he felt eased and for a while seemed better. He then spoke freely with his friends and at last showed his nobility by not excusing himself or accusing his adversary of having acted in any way dishonourably towards him. But though he lived for some hours, it was soon clear that he could not long survive. In fact, he died before the sun went down on the evening of the encounter.

This was the story told by the papers discovered at The Haining and sent by Pringle to Raeburn on January 30, 1840, one hundred and thirty-three years after the contest. Was it also more or less the same story that was told by the papers found at Lessudden some four years later?

That night his family removed the laird of Raeburn's body to Lessudden, and the next day they laid him in the family burial place in the grounds. The economically minded will be glad to learn that due care was taken to see that the family should not be over-charged by the undertakers and John Hoppringle of Torsonce was consulted. He thus advised the Scott family:

'Sr ate Sr. Patrick Scott's desire I have spake to the bearer anent the Hearse at your nephew's buriall, he asks 30 lib. for himself and a dollar to the servants, which compared with Andrew Browns pryces, of which I have some experience, is easier, considering he was ate all the charges of passing the water and feeding at Selkirk. I used any interest I had with him to be easier and found I could not obleidge him to take less without his thinking I imposed on him, which I could not do in this case. He stands in need of money so I must recommend him to you when your convenience serves . . .[1]

A considerable company of friends and relatives assembled for the occasion, and we are fortunate to have the receipted bill for their entertainment.[2] The total cost amounted to £40 13s. 6d. Some interesting items in the account are 'a mitchken* of brandie 12/–', 'Sent to Lasudden 2 dozen clearott 18–00–00', '6 pynts of Sok [?Sack] 8/–', '4 wine glasses 20/– 2 brandie ditto 8/– 1–9–00', '3 Bread 00–13–00'.

But we must leave the Scotts at their funeral repast at Lessudden and turn to poor Mark Pringle, who was in dire peril. Though he had been provoked into the quarrel, he could all the same be proceeded against for murder. Yet no proceedings were ever taken against him. Why was this?

Fortunately for Mark, the Pringles were influential people and this was the age of privilege. Mark's brother John was a distinguished lawyer and for long a member of parliament for Selkirkshire. It was he who had bought The Haining estate a few years previously, and when many years later he was raised to the Scottish bench he took the judicial title of Lord Haining. This John Pringle, it seems, had friends in high places. 'I have heard it said', wrote Alex. Pringle to Raeburn in 1840, 'that Lord Hayning (being MP for the county both

---

* A fourth part of the old Scots pint, or about three-quarters of an imperial pint.

before the Union and afterwards in the British Parliament) from his personal and political friendship with Sir Robert Walpole, got his *Brother's Pardon* very easily managed!!!':[3] and among the papers found at The Haining in 1840 was a letter from Sir James Steuart of Goodtrees, the Lord Advocate, to the Secretary of State, Lord Loudoun, which clearly shows the reluctance of the authorities to act.[4] This is confirmed by the opinion of another lawyer, Robert Pitcairn,* who after studying the papers wrote thus nearly a century and a half after the duel:

> 'From the whole complexion of the case, it is clear to me that the authorities winked at the escape of Mark Pringle, and consequently there could be no proceedings before the High Court of Justiciary. . . . Sir James Stewart, then Lord Advocate, seems to have addressed his letter to the Secretary of State [then Hugh Campbell Earl of Loudoun] who in his turn was bound to report to the Privy Council who would perhaps order the examinations to be recorded—but Pringle having fled, the matter would there be allowed to drop.'[5]

Does this perhaps mean that the authorities were sympathetic towards Pringle because of the conduct of his adversary? It looks remarkably as if they thought that young Raeburn had brought about his own destruction, and that the unfortunate Pringle was the victim of circumstances and should therefore be given all the assistance in their power.

Mark Pringle had in fact escaped to Spain, where he is said to have been captured by the Moors and sold into slavery. After some years of great hardship he seems to have escaped from his captors, for later he is found set up as a prosperous merchant in Spain where he made a large fortune. Mark was twice married and is said to have had three children by each wife. He subsequently became British Consul at Seville and

---

* Robert Pitcairn (1793–1855), antiquary and miscellaneous writer, published *Trials before the High Court of Scotland* (3 vols.), which attracted the attention of Sir Walter Scott.

San Lucar. Eventually he returned to his native Scotland and bought from James, son of James Justice, Clerk of the Scottish Parliament, the estate of Crichton in Midlothian with its famous castle. The rest of his life was passed in retirement, either at Crichton, where he farmed the estate, or in London where he died in 1761, having survived the duel with Raeburn by some fifty-four years.[6] The dead man's widow, who remarried twice—her third husband being Henry Makdougall of Makerstoun—died in 1793, thus surviving her first husband by over thirty years.

One of the decisions come to at the clan gathering at Lessudden after the tragic encounter in Raeburn's Meadow was that the dead man's uncle Walter should act as guardian—'tutor' is the Scottish term—to his children.

The first thing was to choose a school for young Raeburn, and Beardie, who was certainly no scholar, consulted his kinsman, Sir Patrick Scott of Ancrum, '. . . As to Raeburn's schooles . . .' replied Sir Patrick, 'the place being wholsom, affords good deyett, is the Capital of the shire where his residence is and whole estate lays. The Master on[e] of the best in the Kingdom the shollars his relations and neighbours, the house near his Mother, has two ants residing in the place. I shall add no further having fermerly wrote his Mother to the same purpose. . . .'[7] But if Beardie was not up in scholarship he was knowledgeable about money matters and the choice of him to look after the affairs of the fatherless children would seem to have been happy, for many of Walter Scott's accounts are still extant and they showed that he had a methodical mind and an appreciation of the value of money. Moreover, he had for some time been administering the affairs of his own children and other young members of the family. Thus we come across such items as money left with his wife some of which was to be given to 'the scoole master at Candlemas for Walter'; twenty-nine half-crowns and a sixpence and three half-pennies to pay his 'niece Isabelles rent'; forty shillings given 'to Jo Scott my nephew'; 'a loan given to Lillie my daughter' (how much is not disclosed); money left some for his wife and some for Raeburn's wife, as well as scissors, combs, cambrick and holland; for Raeburn such items as 'a wigg £7:4:0, ane Arithmetik book 12/–, 2 lb. tobbacco £1:8:0, 2 dozen pipes 4/–'; We also have an account dated September 10, 1700 headed 'Given to my daughter Isabell qu* they went . . . to Jedr. to pay the taillior 20 shillings . . .'; sent to Sister Menzies** in Edr. 'a fatt cow and a teviotdale boll of oatmeal. I had sent befor a half boll malt and some cheese and onions'; and 'son Walter bought a cow at a roup† and father repaid him'. Clearly 'Beardie' was an indulgent parent. Thus we have an account dated September 10, 1700 headed 'Accompt of Money given out for my Son Walter Scott since the 10 September 1700', when Walter was about seventeen, that contains such items as 'for a pair of gloves 12/– Scots'; 'for an pair of Stirrops and Ireons 16/–'; 'for straw to his Horse 18/–'; 'for an fou†† of oats 24/–'; 'for an pair of Shoes to his man 24/–'; 'for shoes for his horse 15/–'; 'for two girths 10/–'; 'for an Horse comb and brush 20/–'; 'for a scabert to his sword 10/–'; 'for his Periweigs powdering 24/–'; 'for his man's fee 3£.4/– Scots'; 'for 9 capfulls§ of Oats at 4/– the capfull 1£.16 00'; 'for an pair of Gloves 20/–'; 'for his weigs powdering 6/–'; 'for 1 pair of scarlet silk stockins at 10/– starling§§ 0600 00'; 'for his Dancing Master 01 00 00'.

We are fortunate enough to have also some of the accounts

---

* When.
** His sister Christian married James Menzies fourth son of Alexander Menzies of Culterallers in Lanarkshire. She died at Lessudden February 22nd, 1717. William Scott's Memorandum Book NLS MS 3842.
† Auction.
†† Bushel.
§ As much as a cap will hold.
§§ Obsolete form of sterling.

that show how 'Beardie' fulfilled his task as guardian to young Raeburn and his sisters. There is an account—'Walter Scott, Tutor to Raeburn, debtor to Charles Ormston, junior for Raeburn's use', which runs as follows:

3rd	Pr. Arthur Kerr 7 yrds. fine grey	
1720	Eng. Drugget @ 2*s*. 9*d*. pr. yd.	£0 = 19 = 3
	3 yds. & a half Blk. Searge @ 16*d*. pr. yd.	£0 = 4 = 8
	2 dozen & 10 fine Basket work Coat Buttons @ 5*d*. pr. dozen	£0 = 1 = 2
	8 small Buttons: 1½*d*. 3 drop Silk: 4*d*. Canvas 1¼*d*. 1 oz. Thread 2*d*.	£ = = 8¾
	1 ounce & 1 drop fine 3 Cord Mohair @ 8*d*. pr ounce	£ = = 8½
	Half a yd. Buckrom: 6*d*. 1 yd. best Plying: 6*d*.	£ = 01 = 0
	1 pr. fine long Blk. Stockins @ 2*s*. 6*d*.	£ = 02 = 6
12th	Pr. Arthur Kerr's order. 2 doz. 3 Cord Small Blk. Buttons 4*d*. Half an ounce Blk. Thread :1*d*.	£ = = 5
	1 drop Blk, Silk 1¼*d*.	£ = = 1¼
6th	Pr. Arthur Kerr 4 yds. fine	
1720	London Cloth @ 14*s*. pr yd.	£2 = 16 = 0
called	6 yds. & a half Stirling Shalloon	
August	@ 18*d*. pr. yd.	£ = 09 = 9
4th.	2 yds. best plain Fustian @ 16*d*. pr. yd.	£ = 02 = 8
	1 yd. Eng. Buckram: 12*d*. a qtr. yd. Canvas: 3*d*. Stay Tape: 1*d*.	£ = 01 = 4
	1 yd. & a half Eng. Plying: 9*d*. 1 yd. & a half Broad Tirret Ribbon 4½*d*.	£ = 01 = 1½
	2 drop Silk: 10*d*. 2 ounces fine Thread: 6*d*. Button Mountes: 3½*d*. 1 skin for Pockets 8*d*.	£ = 02 = 3½
	1 pr. London Stockins @ 2*s*. 8*d*.	£ = 02 = 8
Sept.	Pr. Arthur Kerr: 1 pr. Stockins	
22nd.	@ 2*s*. 2*d*.	£0 = 02 = 2
	1 yd. & a qtr. Scarlet Stript	

Ticken @ 20*d*. a yd.	£0 = 02 = 1
Button Moulds: 1*d*.	£0 = 0 = 1

Sum Total of the above is—£5 = 10 = 8½

Kelso, Octr. 22nd. 1722.

Received from the above Walter Scott by the hands of
his son Robert, full payment of the above Accompt, and
therefore discharges the same and all preceedings pr. me.

CHARLES ORMSTON Junior.

There is another account from Charles Ormston junior for
Robert's sister, that runs thus:

1721	Walter Scott, Tutor to Raeburn . . . Debtr. 2:	
2nd	To Charles Ormston junior for	£ *s*. *d*.
mo:	Raeburn's sister pr. Arthur Kerr.	Sterling.
called	8 yds. Green Eng. Callimanco*	
April	@ 20*d*. pr. yd.	£0 = 13 = 4
19th.	1 ounce & 1 drop Green Sewing Silk @ 22*d*. pr. ounce	£0 = 01 = 11½
28th	5 yds. & a half Blue & White Sarsnet** @ 2*s*. 9*d*. pr yd.	£0 = 15 = 1½
	4 yds. & a half fine Blue Shalloon† @ 18*d*. pr. yd.	£0 = 06 = 9
	Half an ounce Green Silk: 11*d*.	
	2 drop Blue Silk 3*d*.	£0 = 01 = 2

Sum is—£1 = 18 = 4

Kelso: October 22nd. 1722.

Received from the above Walter Scott by the hand of
his son, Robert full payment of the above accompt, and
therefore discharges the same and all preceedings pr. me.

CHARLES ORMSTON Junior.††

---

* Calamanco: 'A woollen stuff of Flanders, glossy on the surface,
and woven with a satin twill and chequered in the warp, so that
the checks are seen on one side only; much used in the 18th
century' (OED).

** Sarsenet: 'A very fine and soft silk material made both plain

These bills probably saw the end of great uncle Walter's guardianship, for Raeburn and his sisters must have come of age at about this time. And apart from that 'Beardie' was growing old and had only another seven years of his life before him. At any rate in July, 1724 'David Muirhead, Surgeon' rendered his 'accompt' direct to the laird of Raeburn. The total of the doctor's account was £3 19s. 6d. and it covered the period from March, 1724 to May the following year. It included such items as 'vomitting powder', 'Stomackick Tinture', 'syrup', 'cinamon water', 'a vomiting powder to yr. sister Mrs Isobell', 'a dose purging pills to yr. sister', and (regrettably) 'the purging pills renewed to your sister'. Poor Isobel must have suffered from her stomach, for these unpleasant remedies were renewed for her by Dr Muirhead with monotonous regularity in his various statements. [8]

When 'Beardie' Scott died in 1729, he left three sons: the eldest, Walter, who had married Barbara MakDougall, emigrated to America and is believed to have died there without male issue; the youngest, William, 'father of James Scott, well known in India as one of the original settlers of Prince of Wales's island', [9] had a large family. Between them came a third brother, Robert. He as a young man became a sailor, but being shipwrecked near Dundee took such a dislike to the navy that he could never be prevailed upon to go to sea again. This was not the sort of thing that his forceful father could approve, and the furious 'Beardie' refused his

---

and twilled, in various colours, now used chiefly for linings; a dress made of this' (OED).

† Shalloon: 'A closely woven woollen material chiefly used for linings' (OED).

†† NLS MS 2890, ff. 208–10. For earlier accounts between William Scott of Raeburn and his uncle Beardie Wat from 1707 to 1717 see NLS MS 2891 and for Beardie's notes and memorandum Book see NLS MS 2892. The dating is given in old style when the new year started on March 25th and March was regarded as the first month of the year. Thus April was the second, May the third, August the sixth, and September the seventh month.

son any further assistance. Fortunately for him, Robert found a good friend in John Scott of Harden, by whom he was granted a lease of Sandyknowe. Here he settled down and in 1728 took to wife Barbara, second daughter of Thomas Haliburton of Newmains. It was through her that the descendants of the couple have the right of burial within the precincts of Dryburgh Abbey.* When Robert died forty-seven years later he left four sons and four daughters. His eldest son, Walter, born in 1729, at the age of twenty-nine married Anne, eldest daughter of Dr John Rutherford, professor of medicine in the university of Edinburgh, and his first wife, a daughter of Sir John Swinton of Swinton. Walter and Anne Scott had no less than thirteen children, some of whom died in childhood. Their seventh son, born on August 15, 1771 in a house at the head of the college Wynd, Edinburgh, was the most renowned of all the great family of Scott, the future Sir Walter Scott of Abbotsford.

---

* Only three families have this right—the Erskine Earls of Buchan, the Haigs of Bemersyde and the Scotts of Abbotsford.

CHAPTER FIVE

William Scott's Letter Book

Y OUNG William Scott, who had become laird at the age of three on the death of his father in 1707, married late in life. It was not until he was forty years old that he found the wife to suit him. She was Jean, 'eldest lawful daughter of the deceased Archibald Elliot sometime of Mertoun'. They were married on July 18, 1743. Unfortunately for the bridegroom it was an 'irregular and clandestine marriage' and Raeburn was forced to pay a fine for his imprudence.[1] Apart from that we know little of the couple save that William died in his middle sixties in 1769 or 1770. He left two children, Anne born on May 22, 1744 and Walter on August 8, 1748. Neither of his sisters married, and both Isobel and Elizabeth* died within a few days of each other at the end of May 1747. Both left bills for their brother to discharge, some of which are worth recording. Thus

Accompte Mis Bell Scot to
John Pringle, Silk Dyer.
Edr. Novem. 21st 1744.

	£	s.	d.
To an Italian silk gown dyed quaker colour**	= :	3 :	—
To a Stamin† lining dyed the same colour	= :	1 :	—
To a Brocaded silk gown dyed cloth colour	= :	3 :	—
	= :	7 :	—

---

* Keith Scott in *Scott, 1118–1923* calls the second daughter Anne, but this does not seem to be correct.
** A drab or grey colour.
† A kind of woollen or worsted cloth.

This was receipted after Isobel's death:

> June 18　Received this the above Accot. in full payment
> 1747　　and the and the [*sic*] same is discharged with
> 　　　　all preceding this date.
>
> Jo: Pringle

We also have the account of Isobel Scott's surgeon Mr John Douglas, in which such items appear as a melilite* plaister, a cordial and anodyne mixture, a small bundle of white mustard, a glass of sacred tincture, a bundle of valerian tea, and a bundle of purging material. This account was also paid by Raeburn in June 1747, after his sister's death.

Isobel seems to have lived in some sort of a Home in Edinburgh for a time before her death, for we have two accounts from a Mrs Gordon 'Residenter in Edinburgh', in the first of which appear such items as 'Rent from 28th March last to the 29th May current at which time Mrs Scott died being 9 weeks at two shillings sterling per week 18*s*.: To maintenance and Borrowed Money during the said space £1:19:1: To one pound of Candles—0:0:6.: To given in Loan to her for which I have a gold Locket and two gold Rings in pledge—£1:3:0.' Poor Isobel was clearly hard up. Mrs Gordon's second account has such items as 'To given to the Express sent Mr Scott acquainting him of his sister's death—0:1:0.'; 'To a match-kin** of brandy—0:1:0.'; 'To seven pynts of ale—0:1:2.'; 'For Seed Cake—0:1:4'; 'To two Bottles more of wine—0:4:0'; 'To another choppen† of Brandy—0:2:0'; 'To a Loaf—0:0:6'; 'To a gallon of two Pence Ale—0:1:4'; 'To another gallon of Ale—0:1:4d.' 'To the woman who brought the Mort Cloath—0:0:2'; 'To another matchkin of Brandy—0:0:2'. All this was paid for by Raeburn after his sister's death, and Mrs Gordon's

---

* 'A silicate of calcium, aluminium and other bases, found in honey-yellow crystals' (OED).

** The fourth part of the old Scots pint, or about three-quarters of an imperial pint.

† Same as a chopin, a Scottish liquid measure, equal to a Scottish half-pint, or about a quart of English wine measure.

discharge is phrased in delightfully pompous, longwinded legal jargon.

'I Helen Gordon, Indweller . . . at Edn.' Have just now received from Robert Scott in Sandyknow in name of Wm. Scot of Raeburn the sume nineteen pounds nineteen shillings and four pence sterling in full of the above account and for all other accompts Bills and every thing whatsoever that I can pretend was owing to me by the deceast Miss Isobell Scott sister of the said William for whatever cause or occasion att the time of her death or in relation to her funeralls, and I discharge the said William and all others the Representatives of the sd. Miss Isobell of all debts and demands whatsoever on her account. In witness whereof I have . . .

and so forth, and all this is signed by Helen Gordon, before two witnesses.

We also have Isobel's funeral expenses[2] which came to £39 19*s.* 9½*d.* and included: 'To Mr Baillie Wright and Mrs Ronaldson for coffin and grave clothes—acct. discharged— £10:6:6*d.*'; 'For the Horses etc. in Mrs Elliot's—0:8:3'; 'To Raeburn att Lauder—0:11:0'. Elizabeth's funeral expenses, on the other hand, were far more moderate and only amounted to £10 6*s.* 6*d.* in all: they are headed: 'Edr. 30 May 1747. The funerals of Miss Elizabeth Scott Dr. to William Baillie Wright' and include such items as 'To the Warrant for Breaking ground—£0:15:0'; 'To the mortecloath and Ribbons—1:1:0'; 'For the gravemen—0:7:0'; 'To 4 Ushers—1:0:0'; 'To six bearers—0:9:0'; 'To 4 Battonmen 0:4:0'; 'To the Bellman— 0:4:0'; 'To the Recorder—0:2:6'; 'To the poor house— 0:3:0'; and 'To the Coffin cover'd black—3:0:0'. But possibly the sisters were buried together and part of the expenses of the funeral of one of them really applies to the other.

The two children of William and Jean Scott married two of the eight children of Robert Scott, the tenant of Sandy-

knowe. Walter, who on his father's death became the fifth
Raeburn, married Jean by whom he had six children; Walter's
sister Anne married Jean's brother Thomas, Robert Scott's
second son, by whom she had one son. Of Walter and Jean's
six children, three went to India, William the eldest as a
merchant, and Robert and Hugh in the naval service of the
India Company. Robert died unmarried in 1837 at the comparatively early age of sixty-three. Hugh married Sarah,
daughter of William Jessop of Butterley Hall, Derbyshire
and settled near Derby at Draycott House, where he died in
January 1852 aged seventy-four. They had no children, and
Hugh left his property to his nephew William Hugh Scott,
fourth son of the sixth Laird of Raeburn, who married Sarah,
eldest daughter of Alfred Fellows. William Hugh died in
1906 leaving two sons and two daughters. Walter, the fourth
son, never married and died in the West Indies in 1802; and
John the last child became a Major in the 8th Bengal N.C.
and died unmarried in 1832. The only girl in the family,
Barbara, did not marry.

We shall in due course hear more of all the family; but
William, the eldest, will play a particularly prominent part in
our story, so it is fortunate that we have his letter book from
India for the four years 1797 to 1800*. In the first of those
years he was financially embarrassed and in poor health. 'In
this predicament what I have to do is to try next year to get
unconnected and not run the risque of encreasing debts; if
this can be accomplished it is most likely I will pay you a
visit . . .' he wrote to his parents in November, adding 'I am
quite disgusted with this damned place and wish myself
amongst you being while I now write confined to my room with
no slight symptoms of the liver . . .'[3] The same day he wrote
plaintively to his sister Barbara that he was surprised at the
family complaining that he did not write, and then he listed the
letters he had written to his father, his mother and to other

---

* NLS MSS 2896, 2897. This reference covers all quotations from
the letter book.

members of the family. Then he went over to the attack. 'You write me of Walter having gone to Musselburgh and that John is to be a farmer: When will the young gents favor us with a letter. If they cannot write they never will learn sooner and if they can write they shew very little attention to their elder brother in not corresponding. This fault, my dr. sister,' he is careful to add, 'can neither be laid agt. you or our mother: on the contrary I pay you the comp.: of yr being good correspondents.' Then he banters Barbara thus: 'I have a letter from C.E. who says C. is still C. I suppose B. is still B. Pray dr. ladies when will you be wives. You will be aunties soon and ye title of Old Maid annexed to your names. Take the example of Jean Stewart when it is in yr. power and don't hold your head too high—a good advice. . . .'[4] At the same time he complained, as he was fond of doing, of his liver and of being 'much reduced'.

Eleven months later he wrote two long letters from the Cape of Good Hope to his brother Robert. 'My Dr. Bob, I sit down to write you a very long letter which will amuse you for a leisure hour and will begin with a short accnt. of the voyage. We sailed from Penang the 15th July and arrived in Acheen Roads on Ye. 21st. . . . On the 22nd we sailed and after rounding Acheenhead . . . we had nothing but light airs and calms.' In mid-August they got a 'fresh trade' which enabled them to jog along to Mauritius; and so on at great length.[5] In a second letter written a fortnight later he refers inevitably to his health. 'For the first month after leaving Penang I was very ill . . . but after that gradually became better and tho' [I] have now nearly regained my wonted appearance yet my side still complains altho' nobody can live more temperately than I have done. . . .' However, this had not prevented him from having had an amusing four-day excursion with a pleasant party about thirty or forty miles up country. In the company were a Miss Clark and her brother, a Captain Broughton, a Captain Lambert, and 'The Honble. Patrick Stuart, Capt. of the 28th Light Dragoons and son of Ld. Blantyre'. Unfortunately Scott had the misfortune to sprain his ankle when stepping from the side of the ship and 'was confined to a waggon drawn by six capital steeds—the others were on horseback. Broughton is as pleasant a companion as I ever met with and we have laughed immoderately. Capt. Lambert is the same in all Countrys, as good a fellow as ever breathed, he has been very friendly to me indeed.' There is no comment on the Honble. Patrick Stuart or on Miss Clark and her brother. We then have a passage with a very modern touch. 'I shall be completely ruined at this damned place and wish we were gone, you can form no idea of the enormous price of everything, living alone is 3 dollars per day. I will be much agst. my wishes necessitated to draw on Mr Scott for a considerable sum to whom [I] am doubly indebted and obliged beyond my present ability to repay.'[6] This is precisely what he did a few days later, adding that 'we sail tomorrow and I am glad of it for this place is not the climate for livers'.[7]

Three weeks later he reported to brother Bob that they had sailed from the Cape on the 4th in the *Sphynx* and arrived in St Helena Bay on November 17th. 'The *Stately* with Ld. Macartney* and suit is expected here about the beginning of next month to convey us all home—there are about 20 sail here now', adding characteristically, 'St Helena is the worst of all places and it is so very expensive that we have set agoing a Mess on board the *Phenix* which we were glad to find safe here upon our arrival'.[8] So William Scott sailed for home with Lord Macartney in the *Stately* and was soon reporting from Lessudden to James Scott in Penang that his children, James and Bob, who had been left at home in charge of his sisters, 'are reading Vergil at the high School and stand high in their class and in ye opinion of their masters . . . all agree that they have been brought up in ye most becoming manner and give your sisters the merit due': adding 'My Mother begs

---

* George, first and last Earl Macartney (1737–1806) diplomatist and colonial governor, had in December 1796 been appointed Governor of the colony of the Cape of Good Hope, but he was forced by ill-health to resign in November 1798.

her compliments to you. She is much disappointed in yr. not coming home—she wished to thank you for your kindness to her children, but now despairs she will live to see you here'.[9]

But William did not stay long in Scotland for he could not get on with his father and this made Lessudden an uncongenial home. So some eighteen months later we find him writing to his uncle Robert Scott at Rosebank, Kelso, announcing his safe arrival at Fort St George, and commenting somewhat acidly on relatives and acquaintances.

> My brother has a ship I think called the *Clyde* of about 300 tun [*sic*] ½ his own property ½ the houses and only sailed hence 8 days before my arrival—he has been most successful lately. Cousin Bob I learn is in Bengal waiting for a passage to England. Accounts of his conduct it grieves me to say [are] far from flattering. Sir George Leith . . . is counted very morose and uncommonly silent—going to the devil drinking and keeping low company. Marquess Wellesley* travels under greater state than His Majesty. On good authority I have been told he only spoke here to Lord Clive**—even people that dine with him he never speaks to . . . little can be expected from such a character.[10]

To his mother he wrote a couple of weeks later with all the family news. 'After a very pleasant voyage we arrived here. . . . My good Bob only sailed hence 6 or 8 days before we arrived—he is in perfect good health and has been wonderfully successful. The ship he commands it seems is half his own property. . . . John was unwell and left Calcutta and is now at Penang quite recovered. He must be a Lt. long ago as ye promotion has been great and James Scott is in good

---

* Richard Colley, Marquis Wellesley (1760–1842), elder brother of the Duke of Wellington, was Governor General of India at this time.
** Edward, second Baron Clive (1754–1839), eldest son of the famous Robert, Baron Clive (1725–1774). The second Lord Clive, who was Governor of Madras at this time, was created Earl of Powis in 1804.

health still meditating on his voyage home. . . . You will be pleased to hear from me that the accounts I have received here of the success of our mercentile concern are most flattering. Cousin Bob is at Calcutta and I hear intends visiting home.' He was living, he told his mother, with a Captain Spottiswoode 'a most worthy man, his kindness to me has gained him my best esteem'. Amongst his acquaintances was a John Beddell 'who is a fine lad: he was kind enough to offer me a couch in ye country but as I don't like travelling in a palanquin I declined it. . . . When I get to P[enang] which I hope will be all this month you and Barbara shall have a very long letter from me. . . .' Then he wrote pathetically: 'I will be glad to hear how my father comes on and whether he thinks better of me than he did', adding significantly: 'Next time I visit home I shall be more independent or remain where I am tho' at the hazard of my health. I am perfectly pleased with my present prospects and soon expect to be comfortably settled at P[enang] where I hope to enjoy good health. Since leaving and now I have had little reason to complain.'[11] Clearly he did not intend for the future to submit so supinely to his father's will as he had done in the past. At the foot of this letter appears a note in William's hand showing that he kept his word and wrote a long letter to his sister Barbara on August 25, just over a month later.

We have heard much of William's difficult financial position. The same plaint is constantly heard: everything is so expensive that he cannot afford the ordinary comforts of life. The truth seems to have been that William's father was an obstinate, cantankerous and mean man, that he showed his children very little affection and refused to give them the financial help that they felt they were entitled to expect from their parent. Thus as far back as 1793 we find William writing to an uncle who was a lawyer in Edinburgh asking if he could manage to get him a clerkship in a solicitor's office. His uncle replied that he had spoken to a Mr Archibald Lundie who gave him some hopes and promised a final answer on Monday. 'If he agrees I think you will be very well put up, only you must not expect that the gains at first starting can be very considerable. As to boarding that is attended wt. much expense, the lowest board is £25, but mostly £40, but many young men take a room and provide their victualls . . .'[12] But he will not settle the question of board until his relative comes to Edinburgh, which he should do as quickly as possible.

The name of the uncle giving this sage advice was Walter Scott,* and he was a Writer to the Signet. Walter Scott, ws, had a son, also Walter, and a friendship soon developed between the cousins. This was of great importance to Willie in the years ahead, for in due course Cousin Walter became Sir Walter Scott, first baronet of Abbotsford, the greatest of his line.

---

* This Walter Scott's sister, Jean Scott of Sandyknowe, was the wife of Walter Scott of Raeburn. She was therefore Sir Walter Scott's great-aunt.

II
SIR WALTER SCOTT AND
THE SCOTTS OF RAEBURN

CHAPTER ONE

The Cousins

UNFORTUNATELY we do not know what, if anything, came of Willie's application to Walter Scott, ws: all we do know is that the friendship between him and his cousin endured, and some eighteen months later Walter was writing to 'Dear Willy', by this time in India. 'I am happy to hear your passage was pleasant and that you escaped the French cruisers, for tho' a Battle might have given you an opportunity of displaying your valour at their expence, yet I think upon the whole it was as well avoided.' Then he gave all the family and local news: the death of Lizzy Scott; the Harden and Thirlestane ladies well—'I shall not fail to remember you to them when we meet'; his twenty-seven-year-old brother John had obtained a Company in the 2nd Battalion of the 78th and expected to sail for India. From family news he turns to public affairs and reflects the Briton's fear of invasion from the rising power of France following the holocaust of the previous year. 'You will learn by the news papers the astonishing and melancholy progress of the French arms by which they have acquired Holland so that we must now reckon that nation among our enemies. The gentlemen in this country and in most principle towns are all in arms and formed into Bodies of volunteers properly arm'd and disciplined. My brother Tom* is a grenadier in the Edinr. Regt. of 1000 men which comprehends many people of the first rank and property. You may easily infer from this that we think ourselves in some danger of an Invasion which is really to be apprehended but we are prepared to receive them.' And he closes with the usual comment on the weather. 'We have had

---

* Thomas Scott, born in 1774, so aged twenty one at this time.

for some time the most severe weather ever known in this country, a storm of snow which commenced at Christmas, is still remaining in the country. The roads were for 6 weeks and upwards compleatly impassable so that even the mail coach could not run. I send you this news to comfort you under the other extreme of a tropical sun, and that you may not too much regret Scotland which for some time past has much resembled Siberia and been fit only for the habitation of Russian bears. I remain notwithstanding *warmly* as well as sincerely your affectionate Cousin, Walter Scott.'[1]

The cousins do not seem to have corresponded for some time, for no other letters have been found until 1799 when Walter was appointed sheriff-depute* of Selkirkshire. Earlier in the year he wrote to welcome Willie's return to Britain. Willie had been ill at Penang and had come home to recuperate. 'I see you are not aware of a little incident in my history', he wrote, 'namely that I was married about 14 months ago to a very amiable young woman. Her name was Carpenter. She is a French woman by birth and a ward of the Marquis of Downshire. Your sister Barbara is at present our guest and has been for some time. She will be most happy to see you and as my father's house is very melancholy at present, owing to his very weak state of health,** I hope you will have the goodness to order your Trunk to No. 10 South Castle Street where you shall have a good Bed and a hearty wellcome. I defer all my news till our meeting which I hope will be soon.'[2] We may perhaps infer from Barbara's long stay with Walter and Charlotte Scott in Castle Street that things were not very happy at Lessudden in the days of her father and mother. 'Make my respects to all the family at Lessudden', wrote a nephew from Penang, adding rather unkindly, 'and get Barbara married, there are already too many Scotts old maids.'[3]

In January 1800 William left again for the East after having tried in vain for nearly a year to find a position in this

---

* The chief local judge for a Scottish county.
** He died in April, about two months later.

country to satisfy his needs. 'My wife joins in wishing you a good new year and a prosperous voyage to the East', wrote Walter to the departing traveller, who stayed away for five years. How Willie Scott fared in the East we do not know, but he must have made a little money for (as we shall see) he shortly returned to Scotland, bought a small property, married and settled down, all without assistance from his father who continued in his unnatural ways and his customary follies. '. . . Barbara will give you some account of your father's motions, which I believe are full of perplexity', wrote kindly uncle Robert from Kelso. 'He has now given up your uncle Thomas, the fastest friend he ever had—and I do not know whose advice and assistance he takes . . . but if he takes none the consequences will be ruinous. I am trying to get all my matters settled with him next term or in a few months, by which means I hope to resque my name from being blackened &c. &c . . .'* In these circumstances we can well understand Willie's anxiety, as the eldest son of the family, to return to Scotland. 'So, Bill, you hope to say farewell to the East in the end of the year', wrote his brother John early in 1804. 'Fortunate man. I myself will be thinking of it 20 years hence. Remember me to Bob and all my old friends and acquaintances . . .'[4] In the event Willie returned to England that summer. 'I heartily wish you joy of your safe arrival in Britain, I hope without any intention of again visiting the East', wrote cousin Walter. Then he referred to the sad news of uncle Robert's death. 'He was a man of universal benevolence and great kindness towards his friends, and to me individually,' he told his friend George Ellis** '. . . He

---

* Robert Scott, Rosebank, April 15, 1801 to his nephew William Scott, C/o Fairley, Gilmour & Co., Calcutta. Endorsed in William Scott's hand 'Maxpoffle, May 9th, 1829. This day I committed to the flames many letters of my Dear Uncle and only retained this small packet as a remembrance of a most worthy man. W. Scott.' NLS MS Accession 4894.

** George Ellis (1753–1815), author of *Specimens of Ancient English Poetry, Specimens of Ancient English Romance* and other works. Great friend of Sir Walter Scott.

has distinguished me by leaving me a beautiful little villa on the banks of the Tweed, with every possible convenience annexed to it, and about thirty acres of the finest land in Scotland.' But it had its disadvantages. 'Rosebank is situated so near the village of Kelso, as hardly to be sufficiently a country residence; besides, it is hemmed in by hedges and ditches, not to mention Dukes and Lady Dowagers, which are bad things for little people. It is expected to sell to great advantage. I shall buy a mountain farm with the purchase money, and be quite the Laird of the Cairn and the Scaur.'[5]

In consequence of his unhappy relations with his father, Willie does not seem to have been in any hurry to let the family at Lessudden know of his return, for his sister wrote early in the following year expressing surprise on hearing from him from London. 'Our Mother is in good health but lame as she has been for some time past, the Laird is also in a thriving condition. We have indeed lost our good and valuable Uncle so long ago as in June last . . . you are a legatee by his will for £100 and named as a Trustee so you are come in good time for the execution of your office.' Then Barbara refers a shade bitterly to another sad family event: their brother Walter, the fourth of the five boys of the family, had died in 1802. She had written two years ago to tell them, yet none of the brothers in India had taken any notice. Then she reverts to uncle Robert's affairs. 'Uncle left his sweet spot Rosebank to our cousin the Advocate and (what is a little strange) he sold it tother day to a Mr Scott of Melanie,* the purchase money £4,500.'[6]

'Our cousin the Advocate' had recently moved house. 'Since you left Britain I have given up my cottage and settle during the summer in Selkirkickshire [*sic*] at Ashiestiel** upon Tweedside where you will probably find us . . .' Walter

---

* Francis Carteret Scott, who succeeded to Melanie about 1842.
** Now the home of Vice-Admiral Sir Conolly and Lady Mary Abel Smith.

Scott told Willie. 'But whether in country or town we will rely on the pleasure of an early visit.'[7] This new home, situated on the south bank of the Tweed near Selkirk, which Scott rented at this time, had become available through the death of the proprietor, Colonel Russell, who had married a half-sister of Scott's mother, and because his son, James the young laird, was in India; 'a fine gallant fellow and distinguished as a cavalry officer' as Scott was to describe him in after years.* This very charming property—though by no means large—gave the Walter Scotts much more space than they had enjoyed at the cottage at Lasswade.[8]

Lockhart tells us that the Scotts' removal to Ashiestiel was made possible by Walter's vastly improved financial position from the profits derived from the three volumes of *Border Minstrelsy* published between 1802 and 1803, which had been received with great applause. These, together with the £5,000** received from the sale of Rosebank, his uncle's house at Kelso, and a share of his other property said to amount to some £500, all went, he tells us, to swell the funds.[9] The truth seems to have been rather different. Scott received only £78 10s. 0d. for the edition of the *Minstrelsy*. In November 1802 he parted with the copyright for £500, and it is extremely unlikely that there was much of that left by 1805! Furthermore, the money received for Rosebank was all sunk in James Ballantyne's printing business and yielded no dividends except on paper. The real reason why Scott moved to Ashiestiel had nothing to do with his improved finances. It was due to the fact that the Lord Lieutenant insisted that the Sheriff should live for part of the year in his sheriffdom, and Scott had no alternative to complying with the requirements of his superior.

Meanwhile, as time passed Willie's relations with his father did not improve. Indeed, the son was in something of

---

* *Scott Journal*, I, 29. James Russell subsequently became Major General Sir James Russell, GCB. He died at Ashiestiel in 1859 at the age of seventy-seven.

** Not apparently £4,500 as Barbara Scott had told her brother.

a quandary. He was heartily sick of the East and had no intention of returning. At the same time life at Lessudden had become impossible for him. Furthermore, he was anxious to marry and settle down. His choice was Susan Horsburgh, eldest daughter of Alexander Horsburgh of Horsburgh in Peeblesshire; and fortunately sister Barbara approved his choice. 'Since you must have a wife', she told him, 'I think you could not do better than make your bow to the sweet Susy . . . I will surely make out a visit to you before the Horsburghs leave the County, but do not think I shall go to the Balls, as my gentlemen acquaintances are so few in that qr. I might never get a dance and *so be affronted*, and my Dresses besides would not be *half* gay . . .'[10] In May of the following year Willie married 'the sweet Susy'; and he now resolved to acquire the small property of Maxpoffle, near St Boswells, and to settle down there with his wife. He bought it in July, 1807 from James Newbigging for £2,300* 'Having bought Maxpoffle went there in November and lived in the old house', he recorded nearly forty years later, 'and then began hedging and ditching, trees planting, draining, which occupied my attention for many years.' On June 28—three days after their first marriage anniversary—Susan gave birth to their first child, whom they christened Violet. There were to be eleven more in the next seventeen years. 'My amusements were then hunting with the Mellerstain hounds thrice a week, kept greyhounds being fond of coarsing . . .'[11] A nice life for one who can afford it, but (as we shall in due course see) William Scott burdened with a wife and twelve children could not afford it.

---

* The Disposition is dated July 27, 1807. *Subjects*: ALL and WHOLE the five merk land of Maxpoffle with teinds, etc., comprehending the feuduties and superiorities of those parts belonging in property to John Duncanson and Thomas Stenhouse: Together with the farm and lands of Westquarter then tenanted by Thomas Stenhouse as tenant thereof. For details of the purchase and sale of the property, I am grateful to Mrs J. R. F. McKenzie, the present owner of Maxpoffle.

On hearing of the move to Maxpoffle, his good-natured cousin wrote to offer the services of his 'little page Sandie'. 'Several people here want him', he wrote,

> but I think it is doing a favour both to the boy and you to give you an opportunity of having him as he is really upon the whole a very honest useful boy though sometimes addicted to childish tricks. He can do very well in the house and decently in the stable with looking over. His wages will be five pounds a year, his master finding every thing but shoes. I intend to give him his livery coat which is almost new and all his other clothes, all very decent. If you chuse him to wear these in your service (as the livery agrees) you will allow him two guineas for the use of them besides his wages. I can safely recommend the boy strongly and would wish he was settled with a good master and rather in the country than town.

Then comes a characteristic sentence: 'I long passionately to get to Ashestiel once more, but alas! the prospect is still some weeks distant.'[12]

No difficulties had been anticipated in the administration of uncle Robert's estate, as his affairs were supposed to be in perfect order; but in fact his Trust affairs were not so easily settled as Walter had anticipated, and we find him complaining to Willie some eighteen months later: 'Surely it is more than time that they were settled and we the trustees discharged of our trust ... I can get no answer from Smith concerning the Minutes of our last meeting, and I have to intreat you, as your family has so deep an interest, to call upon him ... and insist to have a copy of these Minutes, for I am satisfied that without some one standing over him our friend the Baillie [*sic*] will not budge a step.'[13] Six months later this tiresome matter had made some progress; but further troubles of a domestic nature were soon on poor Walter's plate.

It was only a few years ago that his brother Daniel had disgraced himself and been forced to emigrate to Jamaica. In writing to George Ellis, whom he begged to give Daniel introductions to people on the Island, Walter tried to cast the blame on a woman with whom Daniel had been associating, a certain Carrie Lamb, daughter of a Selkirk seedsman who became housekeeper at Duddingston House. But when Walter met her as Mrs Thomas Mitchell some years later he spoke well of her.[14] George Ellis in response to his friend's plea seems to have furnished him with letters to a Mr Blackburn, a friend and brother proprietor, 'who appears to have paid Daniel Scott every possible attention, and soon provided him with suitable employment on a healthy part of his estates. But the same low tastes and habits which had reduced the unfortunate young man to the necessity of expatriating himself, recurred after a brief season of penitence and order, and continued until he had accumulated great affliction upon all his family.'[15] The rest of the unhappy Daniel's story can be briefly told. The dissipated habits proved incurable and he finally left Jamaica under a cloud of shame. Broken and dishonoured, he returned to Scotland, where he found shelter and compassion from a loving mother. Daniel died in his mother's house on July 20, 1806 bequeathing his illegitimate son by Carrie Lamb* to Mrs Scott's care. Walter Scott later deeply regretted the harsh attitude that he had adopted towards his brother. Yet he would never refer to Daniel as his *brother* but as his *relation,* and it is to Daniel's credit that Mr Blackburn, who had befriended him in Jamaica, was left in ignorance of his close connection with the famous author until many years later when he was applied to on behalf of Lockhart for information for the biography on which he was engaged.[16]

Nevertheless, Walter Scott took much interest in Daniel's son. Thus in 1809 we find him making enquiries about the child, and reporting to his mother on the little boy's mother and her husband Thomas Mitchell. 'His mother and her

---

* It was afterwards claimed that Daniel and Carrie were secretly married and that William was legitimate, but the boy was alway known as Mitchell, so that was extremely unlikely.

husband are now settled in Selkirk and living in a very decent and orderly manner', he wrote. 'The boy as I learn from all the neighbours is very much attended to and both are greatly attached to him ...'[17] Walter took charge of William and cared for him for as long as he was able.* But he was certainly disappointed with the lad before he emigrated to Canada in 1828.

The disgrace of Daniel was bad enough, but Walter was doomed to face more trouble from his brother Tom. Now Tom was the comic of the family and specially close to his eldest brother. 'I never laughed sae muckle at their father's house in Edinburgh', wrote Scott's friend, Robert Shortreed, as reported by his son in 1824. 'It was just fun upon fun, and who to be the daftest the hail afternoon. Tam was out o'sicht the best laugher I ever met wi' . . .'[18] It was with peculiar sadness, therefore, that Walter was forced to admit that in this brother there was another black sheep of the family. It was all very unfortunate for Tom had shown much promise as a lawyer and had become law agent for the Marquess of Abercorn's** estates around Portobello. Encouraged, no doubt, by this early success he had felt able to settle down, and in December 1799 had married Elizabeth, daughter of David McCulloch of Ardwall, by whom he had a son and three daughters. The son, it seems, had a beautiful voice and 'when a boy at Dumfries, was much admired by Burns, who used to get him to try over the words which he composed to new melodies.'[19] Unfortunately Tom speculated and, finding himself called upon to pay cash, he embezzled some of the estate funds. Threatened with imprisonment for debt (as the law then stood), he had in the summer of 1807 to leave the country. He fled to Canada where he died early in 1823. These unhappy events were a great embarrassment to Walter,

---

* It appears that Daniel's natural son, William, after serving with David Bridges, Clothier in Edinburgh, emigrated to Canada in 1828 and died in poor circumstances in Montreal in April 1869 of cancer of the stomach. He was aged sixty-nine. *Notes and Queries,* 4th Series, III, 171, 273, 344, 346 and 493.

** James ninth Earl and first Marquess of Abercorn (1756–1818).

who was on friendly terms with the Abercorns.[20] Yet he showed much kindness to the widow and children in after years. It also inevitably was a cause of much grief to him. 'I am sorry to tell you', he wrote to his cousin, not disclosing the most discreditable part of the story, 'my Brother Tom has given up business finding himself deeply embarrassed with debts. Although I expected this long, yet it is a dreadful shock when it comes. I shall be a loser in money matters but I hope to no great extent.'[21] Amid all these family worries Scott was writing *Marmion*. By November, however, he was able to report to Heber that '*Marmion* was sorely interrupted in summer by some very unpleasant and worrying business but he is now progressive.'[22] Some measure of this remarkable man's success at this early stage in his career may be gauged by the fact that Constable offered the stupendous sum of a thousand guineas for a work that had not even been started. This munificent offer must have been a great encouragement to the young poet.

Now it must not be thought that William Scott was the only one of Raeburn's sons whom Walter Scott befriended, for amidst all these distractions he found time to write to the wife of Robert Dundas of Arniston, chief Baron of the Exchequer, on behalf of Raeburn's son, Robert, 'a very deserving young man, a Cousin German of mine . . . and bears a most excellent character . . . His father Walter Scott of Raeburn is a Scottish Laird of the old stamp who loves a hunter and a fox chase better than any son he has in the world . . .'* Whilst Walter was doing what he could to help Cousin Robert, Cousin Willie chose to nurse a grudge, real or imaginary, against him for some fancied slight. However, when Hugh Scott, Raeburn's third son, was visiting Scott at Ashiestiel his host expressed regret at Willie's coolness. This was a

---

* Scott, Edinburgh, March 13, 1808 to Mrs Dundas. Scott *Letters* II, 33. Grierson is wrong in saying that Scott's correspondent was the wife of the Lord Chief Baron. She was Mrs Robert Dundas, wife of the President of the Board of Control, afterwards 2nd Viscount Melville.

sufficient cue for his guest to act the part of peacemaker; and he urged upon his wayward brother the wisdom of writing a conciliatory letter to his relative. This Willie did, saying that 'it was and still is pleasing to me to consider that I am fortunate enough notwithstanding the existing coolness to feel proud in claiming you as my near relation not only in regard to your good conduct in private life, but at the same time putting a full value upon you as one of the first Poets of the age we live in, for it is impossible for any man to read your works without admiration of the writer—this from me and from a Raeburn (of which you are one) can be considered as no fulsome, tho' humble praise, for I believe we possess a different character in the world than being lavish in that respect'. He felt that his cousin had not treated him with the regard that he had a right to expect and 'surely you could not expect that I was to force myself upon your notice'. However Willie will be graciously pleased to forgive and forget, 'provided you acknowledge that you never intended to give up my acquaintanceship . . .'[23] Poor grousy Willie, how fortunate it was for him that the magnanimity of the man on whom he was to rely so much enabled him to overlook his cousin's petty absurdities. All the same Walter did not quite trust him. 'We will talk of Raeburn when we meet and I will show you a letter of Willies which I have not yet answered,' he told Charles Erskine. 'I must understand him very plainly before I quite trust him.'[24]

It was only recently that Hugh had returned from the East, and on his arrival in London he wrote for news of the family at Maxpoffle.[25] Two years later Robert also returned home and he and his brother took lodgings together. 'Hugh and me have taken Lodgings at No. 47 Southampton Row, Bloomsbury', he told his eldest brother, 'to which place you had better address your letters . . .'[26] A fortnight later Robert told Willie of his intention to buy a couple of good horses before leaving London for Cheltenham, where he expected to stay for twelve or fourteen days. 'If you think the servant you mention is capable of taking good care of the Horses

send him up and let me know what is to be his wages &c. &c.
If he is a steady man he will answer me much better than
any person that I could get here—besides English servants
do not answer in Scotland.'[27] Having duly drunk the waters
at Cheltenham Robert started his journey northwards by
easy stages. '. . . I am glad you are coming to Longtown to
meet us,' he wrote to Willie recently returned from Harrogate,
'and I shall take care to let you know when we will be at that
place.' He was anxious to reach Lessudden in time to see the
St Boswells Fair, which he had not witnessed for many years.[28]
When he arrived home we do not know, but he and Barbara
visited Willie at Maxpoffle before the end of July. 'Barbara
and me intended paying a visit to Maxpoffle today', he told
his brother, 'but the unsettled state of the weather will not
allow us to venture so far from Home . . .'[29] The next day
was more promising and 'Barbara and me' set out on their
journey.[30]

For some time the cousins Walter and Willie had been
discussing the setting up of a 'plain monument to our valued
Uncle Robert'.[31] Willie, after consulting his mother and
family, agreed to Walter's suggestion for the wording on the
tombstone. Then he returned to his own affairs.

Willie's object in life was, and for long had been, to obtain
some post in the county that would enable him to live comfortably at Maxpoffle with his wife and large family until such
time as his father should be so obliging as to quit this life for
a better. It is probable that Willie would have accepted almost
any appointment in Roxburghshire that would give him an adequate salary for not too much work; but there was one post
that he particularly craved at this time, and that was the
Collectorship of Cess* in the County. Moreover, there was a
likelihood that the position might fall vacant before too long,
for the Collector had been old Major Rutherford of Mossburnford since he retired from the Black Watch early in the
century. True, the old man showed every sign of offering

---

* The land tax in Scotland.

himself for re-election. Nevertheless, he was not immortal, and in order to stand a chance of being considered for the vacancy when it should occur, Willie was anxious to obtain the support of the powerful Buccleuch interest.

His cousin Walter, on cordial terms with the duke,* was as always anxious to help, and might even have been generous enough to lend his cousin some money but for the fact that he had just purchased the property on the Tweed now known the world over as Abbotsford, and this outlay left no liquid resources to spare. But he promised to do what he could with the duke. Willie was almost desperate. 'God knows', he groaned, 'God knows in my present situation with a numerous family rising upon me it would be an act of charity could anything be bestowed upon me, as I am left quite unsupported and obliged to struggle on upon my hard earned little gains . . .'[32] Relations with his father remained unchanged; Raeburn at Lessudden continued stern and unbending, whilst his son at Maxpoffle was getting ever deeper into debt. In January 1812 the Duke of Buccleuch, from whom Willie was hoping so much, died. 'The good old Duke of B. has gone,' he wrote anxiously to Walter, 'and I hope the new Duke** will still preserve his influence in the County.' Then followed the usual request. 'At some season . . . I wish you would mention me, your Cousin, as on the look out for some public situation in Roxburghshire. If a young rising family with only a small pittance to support them, and that gained at the hurt of my health will plead for me the fact is true, for other support have I none—and there is now no relation left that has the ability to aid me but yourself . . .'[33] To this appeal Walter Scott replied firmly. 'The Duke's friendship for me has been great and uniform', he told Willie, 'but your good sense and knowledge of the world will easily make you aware that I cannot without abusing this familiarity and incurring

---

* Henry, third Duke of Buccleuch and fifth Duke of Queensberry (1746–1812).
** Charles William Henry, fourth Duke of Buccleuch and sixth Duke of Queensberry (1772–1819).

an assured repulse request any favour which circumstances may render unseasonable . . .' At the same time he wished that '. . . my Uncle had considered a little the situation of his family before engaging himself if he be really engaged to the other party, since you must feel how difficult it makes it for any friend of yours to prefer a recommendation to his Grace . . .' And he ended his letter on a somewhat sharp note. 'I am very plain on this occasion, my dear Cousin, because I am sensible that without such a distinct explanation I shall have little chance of serving in the quarter alluded to and because it would give me extreme pleasure to bring the heads of my clan and my family together upon a footing of reciprocal kindness and obligation.'[34]

No doubt the good-natured Walter was anxious to bring together the heads of his clan and his family, but what hope had he of achieving this when the head of his family was so unpredictable? Thus at the parliamentary election for Roxburghshire that was held in November when Lord Minto's* son, Lord Melgund, defeated the Buccleuch candidate, Alexander Don,** by seven votes, poor Willie's tiresome father saw fit—perhaps in a fit of pique—to desert the Duke's faction and ally himself with the victorious Minto family.† This naturally infuriated Walter Scott. 'I am returned from the election as sulky as a Bear with a headache', he told his Aunt Christian Rutherford—'my almost sister,'[35] as Scott called her—the day after the declaration of the poll,

for we were most completely beaten—lost the day by seven. I had only two topics of consolation—the one that Raeburn whom the Tods had instigated to the unnatural attempt of running down my vote sunk his

---

* Gilbert Elliot, Lord Minto of Minto, Co. Roxburghshire later Governor General of Bengal and created Earl of Minto, 1751–1814.
** Alexander Don, afterwards Sir Alexander Don, sixth Bt. of Newtondon (1780–1826).
† Less than two years later, in June 1814, Viscount Melgund succeeded his father as second Earl of Minto, and in the bye election held on July 25th Don was elected.

own in the attempt—So the disappointed squire returned
on his grey palfrey over Lilliards Edge[36] voteless and
disconsolate—This comes of being a cats paw to scratch
your friends—The said Raeburn in indiscreet zeal was
not unwilling to have perjured himself concerning some
old transactions between my father and him but I had
fortunately a writing which his friends did not advise
him to place his oath in opposition to—If he had sworn
(which he was most anxious to do) Newgate or the
pillory would have been the word—My other comfort is
that Don spoke most exceedingly well—as much so as
any orator I ever heard in my life and with great propriety,
while Elliot made but a stammer of it.'[37]

In these circumstances how could Walter Scott approach
the Duke of Buccleuch on behalf of the son of the man who
had gone over to the opposition? The situation was awkward
enough, yet Willie begged his cousin to do what he could to
assist him. He assured his cousin that he had for long been
attached to Major Rutherford and so to the Buccleuch family
who supported him. 'I of course did not approve of my
father's siding with the Minto family and deserting the late
Duke and his old acquaintance, Mr Rutherford, notwithstanding my being married to his [Rutherford's] second cousin
which was certainly an additional reason for his being of that
party . . .'[38]

In fact, so pressed was Willie for cash to meet his liabilities
that it looked as if he would have to part with his vote in
Roxburghshire. 'I have mislaid Willie Scott's note', Walter
told the new Duke of Buccleuch, 'he presses for an answer on
the subject of his vote within a few days. I would we could
find a good purchaser—the price is very moderate £600.'[39]
This much perturbed the duke who told his correspondent
anxiously that it was essential that either the vote be disposed
of to 'a steady friend' or means found to enable Willie to
retain the vote, in other words, that the necessary funds
should be advanced to him. 'I have no hesitation in telling
you', wrote the anxious duke, 'that it would be extremely

inconvenient to me at this moment to make any adequate advance. I have had some very heavy demands to satisfy lately, which have left me very *bare*. How far Mr Scott would choose to be so relieved is more than I know . . .'[40] It is said that a wealthy admirer of Charles James Fox, anxious to help him in his financial difficulties, once asked one of the great man's intimates how he thought he would take it if he offered him an allowance. Oh, said the friend, he would take it quarterly. No doubt much the same answer would have been returned by Willie Scott.

Eighteen months later the Prince Regent offered Walter Scott the poet-laureateship. But the laureateship had been made ridiculous by the poetaster who had held the office for twenty-three years. Henry James Pye had been appointed laureate in 1790—perhaps because as an MP he had given unstinted support to the prime minister, Pitt;* certainly not because of his poetry which was utterly contemptible—and until his death in 1813 had produced on the king's birthday and like occasions effusive odes breathing the most worthy patriotic sentiments expressed in language of the utmost banality. Should Walter succeed this feeble songster, 'the poetical Pye',[41] as he contemptuously called him? He consulted the head of his clan, the new Duke of Buccleuch.[42] The duke was decidedly against it. 'I should be mortified to see you hold a situation which, by the general concurrence of the world, is stamped ridiculous', he wrote, '*Walter Scott, Poet Laureate*, ceases to be the Walter Scott of the Lay, Marmion** etc. Any future poem of yours would not come forward with

---

* Pitt's most recent biographer, Mr John Ehrman, admits that 'it was disgraceful—and was so regarded—to appoint the recently retired MP Henry James Pye Poet Laureate in 1791'. Ehrman, *The Younger Pitt, the years of acclaim*, 593. The appointment can be compared to Lord Salisbury's nomination of Alfred Austin in 1896.
** *The Lay of the Last Minstrel* published in 1805 had been followed by *Marmion* in 1808.

the same probability of a successful reception. The poet laureate would stick to you and your productions like a piece of *court plaster* . . . only think of being chaunted and recitatived by a parcel of hoarse and squeaking choristers on a birthday, for the edification of the bishops, pages, maids of honour, and gentlemen-pensioners! Oh, horrible, thrice horrible.'[43] That was enough for the duke's kinsman: Walter Scott declined the laurel.[44]

One person at least was sorry that Scott refused the laureateship, his kinsman Harden. 'It is such a pity you did not agree to be Laureat,' wrote Hugh Scott, 'you would have written such beautiful odes. The Prince has commanded Clerk* to let Him know as soon as you come to town—and He has directed that you are to have the best of his library, whenever you wish to come to it. So you see what great things await you. I hope, however', he added, 'HRH will not insist on your being of his jolly parties . . .'[45] So much for the reputation of the Prince Regent!

Another person who may have regretted Walter's decision was his mother. Old Mrs Scott was staying with Raeburn at Lessudden when he wrote to advise his mother that he would refuse the laureateship. 'As you are so close in our neighbourhood I hope you don't intend to cheat us of a visit . . .' he added, 'Peter** will attend you on any day you please and either return with you to Lessudden or set you forth on your return home whichever you please . . .'[46]

We left Robert and Hugh Scott a few years back having taken lodgings together at 47 Southampton Row, Bloomsbury. By the end of 1813 Robert Scott had decided that he was sick of the fogs and cold of London and that he would, at any rate

---

* Dr James Stanier Clarke (c. 1755–1834), the Prince Regent's Librarian at Carlton House.
** Peter Mathieson, Scott's coachman, brother-in-law of Tom Purdie.

for a time, return to Penang by the *Castle Huntly* due to sail at the end of January. 'In what I mentioned to you one day at Maxpoffle you will not be much surprised at my going out again', he told his brother, 'indeed after considering the matter well it appears to me to be perhaps under all circumstances as good an arrangement as I can make for the present . . .'[47] One wonders how much the unhappy state of things at Lessudden had strengthened Robert's resolve. At any rate his decision was not well received. Raeburn's friend, William Lindsay of Feddinch, told William that he greatly regretted that 'Bob has actually taken his Passage to go back to Penang again . . . I can only feel for his Mother and Father who never can expect to see him again and the affection shown him by his sister will be severely put to the Tack . . .'[48] Robert himself seems to have been surprised at the 'melancholy view' the family took of his pending departure. 'I can assure you that I have considered *not a little* before I came to the resolution of going out again but as I said before it seems to me to be the best place that I can *at present* adopt.'[49]

Four months later Walter received a *cri de coeur* from his cousin William, complaining bitterly as usual of his position and the lack of parental sympathy. 'The fall of interest in India has hurt my little income much, yet notwithstanding I can meet with not the least support from the quarter eldest sons generally have to look to. . . .' Can Walter help, he asks pathetically? The Master of Harriers in the Prince Regent's household is vacant. If any salary attaches to the office, can his cousin obtain it for him? 'I can assure you that nothing but real necessity obliges me to make this request to you, and you well know I have no relation that possesses your influence in the world . . . [I] hope you wont think that in doing so I indent where I have no pretensions.' Then he refers to his father again. 'Thus far have I got on since 1794 on my own footing, almost entirely, and it must appear odd to you that circumstanced as I am now Raeburn has not the least intention of settling a shilling pr ann: on me.' And, in a postscript he adds that his brother Robert, about to sail

again for India, has given him his horse, and as brother John
has given him another he will have one to sell. 'A young 3
year old filly by Orion out of a little Irish mare that was mine
22 years ago and died last year as my pensioner. She is very
handsome and promises not to be high and perhaps when
broke might suit you.'[50] It is hardly surprising that Willie
was not made Master of the Prince Regent's Harriers.

Whilst the family were facing up to the unhappy prospect
of losing Robert, Hugh was deciding to marry and settle
down. He had returned from the East in comfortable circumstances, and had followed this up by successfully wooing a
young heiress. She was Sarah, daughter of William Jessop of
Butterley Hall, Derbyshire, a rich Midlands manufacturer.
'I leave this for Butterley tonight', he told Willie, 'and hope
in a few days after my arrival to call Sarah mine. She is an
amiable good girl and I am sure you will like her. I propose
after marriage to take the tour of the Lakes on my way north
and in all probability will be with you about the 16th . . . As
Sarah is particularly fond of horse exercise could you get
John's mare in order by the time we arrive . . .'[51] The couple
settled down at Draycott House, near to the Jessops and not
far from Derby. Only one thing marred their happiness; they
had no children.

Robert had duly sailed early in 1814, and in October of
that year he sent his brother £100 for the benefit of the poor
of the village of Lessudden. He may either invest the capital
and use the income for their benefit or he may buy a plot of
ground upon which they could grow potatoes or what they
please. 'The sum is trifling', he wrote, 'but I hope it will be
of some use—remember I do not wish my name to be in the
Kelso papers.'[52] It would be interesting to know how Willie
Scott employed his brother's gift.

Two years later, in 1816, fresh rumours were afloat that old
Rutherford was at last contemplating resignation. To Willie's
plea for help his cousin promised to do all he could and to
write to the Duke of Buccleuch. But, alas, that proved fruitless, for the Duke told Scott that he had pledged his support

elsewhere. However, nothing was lost because the whole
matter came to naught. Rumour proved false and Major
Rutherford held on to his collectorship for another five years.
So eighteen months later we find Willie still badgering his
good-natured cousin for help. 'Could you through your good
offices', he asks, 'obtain for me a situation in this Country
the duties of which I may be qualified to discharge with
credit to myself and benefit to my employers . . . ?', all of which
is highly necessary 'from my being unable to obtain any
pecuniary aid from the paternal property which leaves me
in a very unpleasant situation with regard to my finances'.
Then in order to show his qualifications he lists his accomplish-
ments: 1788 to 1793, Clerk to a Writer and Writer to the
Signet; in 1794 abroad, to become a 'Tree Merchant' in the
East Indies. Ill health compelled his return home in 1799,
but in 1800 he recovered and went out again. He remained in
the East Indies for five years but returned in 1805 'in very
bad health and without any fortune'. Thus he had been
actively employed for seventeen years in two different capaci-
ties and given satisfaction to his employer. 'I do not mean to
say', he added modestly and truthfully, 'that my abilities
are beyond mediocrity,' but he promises to work conscien-
tiously at any appointment his cousin might procure for him.
What sort of occupation has he in mind? That is a difficult
question to answer. 'I have sometimes thought of Paymaster
to a Regiment and sometimes I have been even ambitious
enough to consider myself eligible for a Commissioner of
Customs or Excise, but I fear this will be looking too high and
beyond my merits.' In that he is perfectly correct. The Commissioner of Customs received a salary of £600 per annum,
twice what Scott received as Sheriff-Depute. 'At other times
I have thought that from having had ten years acquaintance
with civil matters I might perhaps answer for Steward to
some Nobleman, but then it is not every person that I might
please in this respect . . . I look not to a large Salary but
merely to such an allowance as might enable me to maintain
and educate my family in a suitable manner, something on a

par with that of our progenitors—this is a natural and I hope only a becoming pride suiting a borderer, suiting a Scott . . .'[53]

It was the same old moan, and no doubt Cousin Walter was getting rather tired of Willie's importunities; at any rate he urged him to try to come to terms with his father. 'I hope', he had written two days before, 'the Laird will think better of his very unnatural conduct.'[54] But Walter was too good natured not to do his best to influence the Duke of Buccleuch on Willie's behalf, and he begged him to use his good offices to obtain for Willie the position of British Consul somewhere. 'I send under a separate cover two letters of a painful nature from my Cousin Willie Scott younger of Raeburn', he told the duke. He did so with the utmost reluctance, having told Willie clearly that he did not see how Buccleuch could help. 'I found him however so much disposed to think that I exaggerated these difficulties that I cannot without unkindness to a very near relation and a really meritorious young man avoid transmitting his own statement of his case. His father—if he can be called a father—has at least £1,400 a year clear, of which he spends at least a visible expense of about £300, yet will he allow his son and heir a man (I must scratch out *young*) of unexceptionable character and conduct with an increasing family of seven or eight fine children actually to fly to servitude to support the necessary means of subsistance. I should mention it to Willie's honour that he has positively declined such pecuniary aid as I among many of friends was most willing to have afforded and even pressd on him. Indeed, I do not well see what can be proposed or done for him unless something of a consulship in a foreign country could be obtain. . . .'[55]

But the duke was not encouraging, saying pessimistically that he saw 'nothing but darkness' for Willie Scott. 'From experience', he told his friend, 'I know how difficult it is to procure the situation of Consul. For two years I struggled in vain to persuade Ld. Castlereagh* to give me one not only for

---

* Robert, Viscount Castlereagh, later second Marquess of Londonderry (1769–1822).

Walter Scott V
of Raeburn,
uncle of Sir
Walter Scott

Jean 3rd,
daughter of
Robert Scott of
Sandyknowe,
wife of Walter
Scott V of
Raeburn and
aunt of Sir
Walter Scott

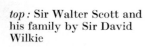

top: Sir Walter Scott and
his family by Sir David
Wilkie

right: Sir Walter Scott
Engraved by H. T. Ryall
from the original by J. P.
Knight

a very old personal friend but also a very old public servant. . . .'[56] If nothing could be done for so influential a man, what hope was there for Willie Scott? So poor Walter Scott, enlarging on the difficulties facing them, was forced to admit that there was nothing more he could do, adding rather feebly, it must be admitted, 'However, you may allways reckon upon my most sincere good wishes and my best services when they can be useful to you.'[57]

Poor Willie was now distracted, and in his anxiety he actually for once did something for himself. In the days before pensions were granted it was not unusual for a new holder of an office to make an arrangement with his predecessor by which he did all the work and the outgoing officer pocketed the whole or part of the salary for life. This is precisely what Walter had done way back in 1806 when old George Home of Wedderburn, who had been a Clerk of Session for twenty-five years, intimated that he would be willing to retire in Walter's favour on condition that he was permitted to retain the emoluments for the rest of his life. Now Willie made that same suggestion to Rutherford. 'Driven to extremity for want of funds to support my youngsters', he told Walter a few days later, 'I have made a proposal in secrecy to Collc. [i.e. Collector] Rutherford': he had asked him if he would be willing to retire in his (Willie's) favour on condition that a certain proportion of the salary was paid to him. He now asked his cousin what, in the event of his agreeing, would be a 'fair proportion' for him to retain. But Walter poured cold water on the whole idea, pointing out that, if Rutherford did agree to surrender about half the remuneration, say £150, he, Willie, would have to pay out the whole of that sum to a clerk, and so would be left with nothing.[58] Further, Walter was convinced that Rutherford would not be amenable to any arrangement that entailed his parting with any portion of his fees; and that therefore they must be content to wait until such time as the old man should at last decide to vacate his office.

CHAPTER TWO

Sir Walter Scott of Abbotsford

IN THE summer of 1818 Charlotte Scott's brother, Charles Carpenter, died leaving his considerable property—at first said to be as much as £40,000, but soon found to be much less—to the Scott children in equal shares after the death of his widow. 'This relieves me in a great measure,' Scott told his cousin, 'from the charge of providing for the younger branches of my family.' It was partly due to his improved circumstances as the result of this legacy that made Scott feel able to accept the baronetcy he was offered at this time. It has long been believed—and was certainly believed by Scott himself—that the honour was the spontaneous and unsolicited gift of the Prince Regent, and that at the prince's decree it was 'to be gazetted singly as a mark of especial favour', as he told his cousin. 'I think you will agree with me that I could not refuse with decency a mark of honour conferred from the immediate and spontaneous wish of the Sovereign, especially as I have enough for myself and the young folks are well provided for'.[1] To his old friend Morritt,* the traveller and classical scholar and the munificent owner of Rokeby Park in Yorkshire, he wrote rather more irreverently. 'There is another thing I have to whisper to your faithful ear. Our fat friend being desirous to honour Literature in my unworthy person has intimated to me by his organ the Doctor** that with consent ample and unanimous of all the

---

* John Bacon Sawrey Morritt (1772?–1843), 'a man', Scott recorded, 'unequalled in the mixture of sound good sense, high literary cultivation, and the kindest and sweetest temper that ever graced a human bosom'.
** Dr James Stanier Clarke.

potential voices of all the ministers each more happy than
another of course on so joyful an occasion he proposes to
dubb me baronet—Remember I anticipate the jest, "I like
not such *grinning* honours, as Sir Walter hath."[2] After all
if one must speak for themselves I have my quarters and
emblazonments, free of all stain but border theft and high
treason which I hope are gentleman-like crimes. . . .'[3]

We now know the truth of the matter, which is very different. It is quite likely that the Prince Regent in later years
after his accession pretended that he had been anxious to
honour his friend, the most famous novelist of his day. But,
if he did, he was only acting true to form, for all the world
knows he was a man who, like Pilate, asked after truth but
did not stay for an answer; and in grossly deceiving his friend,
as it appears likely that he did, he merely treated him as he
treated all who had the misfortune to come within his orbit.
The truth as revealed by the Blair Adam manuscripts is that
it was only after William Adam of Blair Adam,* Lord Chief
Commissioner of the Scottish Jury Court, had worked like a
Trojan in his efforts to persuade the prince to confer the
honour and had pestered ministers of state to pester the
Regent that he agreed after several years of the most intense
pressure.[4] Among the vast number of letters of congratulation
that Scott must have received at this time, one expression of
good wishes must have especially delighted the new baronet.
'I do sincerely congratulate you', wrote his old friend and
chief, the Duke of Buccleuch, 'on the splendid reversionary
fortunes of your children. *It ought not* to be so, but the world
will attach considerable importance to the Circumstance of
wordly wealth, and the knowledge of your Children's more
than independence, will attach a great degree of (false)
colouring to your proposed Rank than all the Triumphs of
St George, St Andrew, St Patrick or all the *Knights* and
Saints of former days were you to achieve them . . .'[5]

---

* William Adam of Blair Adam (1751–1839), son of John and
nephew of Robert and James Adam, the architects.

Walter Scott had to prove his arms and descent, as he told Willie, 'and I wish to do so not only as a member of your family but also as representing through our Grandmother the ancient family of Newmains and having a right to bear their arms quarterly with those of Scott. I will send you my pedigree when I have made it out as we are mutually interested in its being correct and without any erroneous pretensions or inaccuracies . . .'[6]

Thus early in 1820 Cousin Walter became Sir Walter Scott of Abbotsford.

Unfortunately Willie Scott's financial position did not improve, and when it was clear that old Rutherford intended hanging on to his collectorship for some time to come, Sir Walter in February 1819 discussed the matter with William Scott of Teviotbank, ws,* brother of Dr James Scott of Ellem who with his kinsmen settled at Darnlee near Abbotsford and acted as unofficial physician to the laird in his latter days. After much earnest confabulation it was decided that Teviotbank should write to Raeburn formally demanding that he should pay certain interest said to be due to his eldest son. 'I think this must bring him to his senses and shew him that whether he will or no he must do something for you. Indeed, it becomes William Scott's duty to do this in your present circumstances so that it is not a measure of choice but of necessity.' Walter added that, snow permitting, he intended to go to Abbotsford on Saturday or Monday and begged his cousin to come and dine with him on Sunday or Monday, when 'we can talk over this matter and if we can strike out any thing which can be useful for you, it shall not want whatever I can do to bring it to a favourable issue.'[7]

---

* William Scott of Teviotbank, ws (1782–1841). The lairds of Teviotbank, Ellem and Abbotsford were distant cousins, each having the same great-great-great grandfather.

By great ill luck, during the spring and early summer of this year Walter Scott was seriously ill, so that little good seems to have been achieved by Scott of Teviotbank's intervention; and it began to look as if poor Willie would have to sell his house. His friend William Lindsay of Feddinch took a poor view of this. 'The old Laird's conduct to you is certainly not easily to be accounted for', he wrote, 'as he must have been very sensible of your Difficulty with so large a Family as yours. There is a Rich Taylor come from Calcutta to this neighbourhood who I am informed wishes to purchase a Made Place. I will try and meet with him and inform him of yours . . .'[8] Alas, he was negotiating for another property, so nothing came of the matter.

By this time Sir Walter was recovering from his illness: 'My dear Willie, I am once more on my legs and think of being at Abbotsford next week being unequal to any official duty.' Cousin William had offered to accompany the invalid to Yorkshire to drink the waters, but received a typical reply. 'I am much obliged to you for your very kind offer to go with me to Harrowgate but I am no great believer in the virtue of these Spaw waters. For those who seek relief from business and from the ordinary routine of life they may be useful as the society is a relief to the mind. But I am never so well or happy any where as when at home engaged in my own pursuits and with my own family.'[9]

During the later months of that year and the spring and early summer of 1820 the cousins were in constant correspondence on Willie's affairs and his chances of obtaining the appointment of Collector of Cess whenever old Rutherford should retire. But as ill-luck would have it the other candidate in the field was Charles Robson of Samiston,* who was married to Major Rutherford's daughter Martha. This gave him a considerable advantage, for when at last the wily old man at the age of seventy-four decided to retire he confided

---

* Charles Robson of Samiston (1770–1830), later represented by the Robson-Scotts.

his intention to his son-in-law before making it generally known, thus giving him the opportunity of canvassing before the news got abroad. Rutherford had, it seems, tried the same trick once before, then on behalf of one of his nephews; but the news leaked out and Mossburnford was induced to beat a hasty retreat. This time, however, the secret had been better kept, and Robson had fairly stolen a march on the opposition. Nevertheless Walter Scott thought it would be a very close contest, as he told his friend Lord Montagu.*

'I may be a partial judge but I cannot say that I see any comparaison betwixt the Candidates. Raeburn supports [represents] the next cadetship of the Harden line and has long been settled in the County and who Mr Robson's father may be I do not profess to know his grandfather would probably be a riddle to himself. Reaburn [Maxpoffle] has moreover ten children and may have God knows how many more for his wife *will* breed and his father my much honoured [uncle] will NOT die. So there are many mouths and I fear very little meat for the old trojan will not part with a penny though he has an estate of £1,200 a year. I wish to God your Lordship would give us the countenance in this matter which I have every reason to think I should have experienced from my lamented friend** who knew and regretted Reaburn's [Maxpoffle's] situation. He is a complete man of business and most gentlemanlike in his manners and habits of thought and action. Besides I cannot but think that as they all know he was in the field they should not have begun an underhand canvass but have given the County fair play.'[10]

---

* The fourth Duke of Buccleuch had died in 1819 having held the dukedom for only some seven years. The new duke, his eldest surviving son, was only about fifteen at this time, so his affairs were being looked after by his uncle, Lord Montagu (1776–1845), who had succeeded to the barony of Montagu on the death of his grandfather, George, Duke of Montagu. Lord Montagu had only daughters, so the barony died with him.
** The late Duke of Buccleuch.

Two days later, however, he wrote to Montagu again. 'Fair play is a jewel. I wrote to you the other day that I thought that our late dear freind would have countenanced young Reaburn in his present application and this impression is still strongly on my mind'. But on re-reading two letters from the late duke they seem to indicate that he intended to be neutral. 'This is against my request but the truth is the truth and I would not willingly mislead you of all men by the least inaccuracy in my report. The Duke certainly expressed himself favourable to Reaburn upon many occasions.'[11]

Major Rutherford's unfair conduct put the opposition on their mettle and Sir Walter told Willie that he had written on his behalf to Sir Alexander Keith* and to Wauchope of Niddrie. 'I fear I shall find no access to the Bells,** but I will try. They are you know keen politicians and it is possible my interference might do more ill than good. But are there not others whom I might influence and especially in our own corner? You must remember the Commissioners of Supply vote and not neglect the blue-bonnets.† You have only to let me know and I will make every possible exertion in my power. . . .'[12]

Not to neglect the Commissioners of Supply vote was certainly good advice. The Commissioners, set up by the Act of Convention of 1667, were responsible for the general business of the county, and were appointed to collect the land tax in their respective counties for the 'supply' of the Sovereign. In due course additional functions were laid upon them such as providing the police force, preparing the valuation roll, the provision or prisons, or the maintenance of highways, bridges and ferries. The Commissioners were named individually, the qualification being the possession of

---

* Sir Alexander Keith of Dunnottar and Ravelstone (1780–1833).
** Robert Bell (1781–1861), advocate and William Bell (1783–1849), ws, second and third sons of Benjamin Bell of Hunthill, MD. They were related to Scott and both brothers were free holders in Roxburghshire.
† The Lowlanders.

landed property to the annual value of £100. A landowner could be represented by his agent and, if he had over £800 a year derived from land rentals, his eldest son could also be a Commissioner of Supply. Their number also included the Sheriff, the Sheriff-Substitute and various representatives of the burghs of the county.[13] They were therefore persons of importance in the county and their vote was of considerable consequence to any candidate.

Among those whom Sir Walter had canvassed was his close personal friend, John Scott of Gala,* 'one of the kindest and best-informed men I know,'[14] and he begs Willie to come to Abbotsford to dine and sleep in order to meet him. 'I understand Robson says he will head you by 18 which is I think impossible . . .'[15] At the same time he had some hopes that Rutherford, in spite of his manœuvres on his son-in-law's behalf, might be moved to sympathy in Willie's position. 'He knows well enough you have had hard measure but he will not be ready to admit any points which make against his friends and perhaps by agitating such we may indispose him yet further. I think we will have a better chance of making an arrangement with him at Jedburgh than by going on purpose on Saturday which, to be sure, would be a throwing up of the game.'[16] Another kinsman consulted was Hugh Scott of Harden,** who promised his assistance. 'I will stand by you and him to the last', wrote Walter. 'I could breakfast with you on Saturday at 10 and proceed to Jedburgh with my horses . . . But the first thing to know is whether Harden advises peace or war . . .'[17] What Harden advised we do not know.

The contest took place on April 30th. Robson had said that he would win easily, Scott that it would be a close contest. The latter proved the better prophet. In fact Willie lost the collectorship by only six votes, 47 for Robson, 41 for Scott.

---

* John Scott of Gala (1790–1840), married 1820 Magdalen, daughter of Sir Archibald Hope, Bt., by whom he had two sons and two daughters.

** Hugh Scott of Harden (1758–1841), MP, allowed Barony of Polwarth, 1835.

Sir Walter told his friend Lord Montagu that Robson's 'advantageous start' was the main cause of the defeat and vowed they would certainly try again next year with good chance of success. The sad part of the affair from Sir Walter's point of view, he told Montagu, was that his cousin had a very large family and 'such a hard hearted ostrich of a father'.

That father and Sir Walter's eccentric friend Lord Buchan,* it seems, made a comic pair at the declaration. 'Lord Buchan and Old Reaburn', Scott told Lord Montagu, 'the two most absurd figures I ever beheld stuck themselves like two Roman Senators into the two great curule chairs** which are usually occupied by the Lords of Justiciary and thus sublimely seated sate winking like a brace of barn-door owls not understanding a single word of the procedure'. Walter Raeburn, it seems, did not want to attend, pleading by way of excuse that he had a whitloe on his finger. But Sir Walter would not hear of such nonsense, and he threatened—so he told Montagu

> to drag a red herring from Lessudden House to Jedburgh and lay Baillie's hounds on it to hunt a trail which he must needs have followed if there was a breath of life in him. However he came graceful in shawl drapery which supported the whitloe'd finger. The old carrion resentful of some tart usage I had given him in the great contest betwixt Don and Elliot never once spoke or thanked me for all the personal trouble I had taken besides bringing more than a fourth of his son's freinds. I have great hope he will soon give the crows a pudding in which case the devil may wear black for I will get me a suit of sables as Hamlet saith.[18]

Another nine years were to pass before the 'old carrion' gave 'the crows a pudding'. And Scott wrote with equal bitterness to his daughter Sophia, staying with her father-in-law near Glasgow.

---

* David Stewart Erskine, eleventh Earl of Buchan (1742–1829).
** A chair inlaid with ivory and shaped like a camp-stool with curved legs, used by the highest magistrats in Rome (OED).

I have had another mortification in Maxpopple losing his
election for Collectorship of the Taxes by forty one to
forty seven. It would have been about £250 a pretty help
to a poor gentleman with ten children. The disappointment will add a little more acid to a temper already
efficiently sourd with disappointment. That execrable
old carrion Reaburn Senior had a sore finger and threatened to refuse to come to Jedburgh when we were pulling
all oars for his son. At last he and Lord Buchan made
their appearance two such quizzes were near seen on
earth the one ambling and pacing and the other stalking
through the court room they both by joint consent made
their way to the highest places in the Synagogue (two
great elbow chairs on a high bench) and there sate like
the two Kings of Brentford.*

Indeed, the animosity generated in the county by this
election, Scott told his daughter, was prodigious. 'So a post
of £250 a year can make as much dissention among a body of
country gentlemen united by blood friendship and mutual
opinions as the handful of nuts which a mischievious boy
threw on the stage when monkeys were acting a play made
confusion amongst the actors.'**

But, everyone agreed, the contest would be fought again
next year with more prospect of success. So Rutherford—
hoping perhaps to pour oil on troubled waters—wrote to
Scott regretting the ill-will being engendered and pleading
that he had no alternative to supporting Robson who had
'from previous circumstances a right to call upon me . . . Since
it must continue,' he wrote, 'I hope it will be conducted with
liberality and good humour on both sides and that we will not

---

* Like the two Kings of Brentford smelling at one nosegay: said
of persons who were once rivals but have become reconciled.
Buckingham's *The Rehearsal*, II, ii.
** Sir Walter Scott, Abbotsford, May 1st [PM 1821] to Mrs John
Gibson Lockhart, Revd Dr Lockhart, Germiston, Glasgow. Scott,
Letters, VI, 431–2. Lockhart's father was the Rev. John Lockhart
(1761–1842), minister of Carnbusnethan and in 1796 of the
College Kirk in Glasgow.

allow it to interrupt that harmony which . . . has never as yet been interrupted.'[19] But he made no mention, be it noted, of the trick by which he gave his son-in-law an unfair advantage, the real cause of all the friction engendered in the election.

Clearly Sir Walter was thoroughly put out that the weight of his influence combined with the considerable efforts that he had made had not been sufficient to gain his cousin the victory, and it is doubtful if Rutherford's letter lessened his annoyance. In the first place Lord Montagu, from whom Scott hoped for support, had told him that he regarded himself as engaged and that therefore it was useless to press him further. Yet he still had hopes of winning him over: '. . . when he comes down in autumn', he told Willie, 'I do not fear that upon finding the opinions of so many of the Buccleuch party are favourable to you he will be disposed at least not to oppose you. We can scarce expect he will go against the Member.'[20] But that was not the only matter to put Sir Walter out at this time. He was also disconcerted at the discovery recently made that certain persons were claiming that their names should have been inserted in the list of Commissioners of Supply and had been omitted. The MP for Roxburghshire, Sir Alexander Don,* had sent to Lord Lothian, the Lord Lieutenant for the County, a signed list of the persons so affected for him to determine whether or not their names should be included. Don was an intimate friend of Scott and a frequent guest at his table,** and Sir

---

* He had been elected, it will be remembered, in 1814, when the sitting member, Lord Melgund, had succeeded his father as Earl of Minto.

** Scott paid a handsome tribute to his friend when he died aged only forty-seven. The two men certainly had one trait in common— extravagance. Thus when Don died the estate of Newton Don had to be sold on behalf of the creditors. It is said to have produced the large sum of £85,000, but this was insufficient to meet the debts; and the son Sir William Henry Don (1825–62) in a great effort to pay off the sum still owing, some £7,000, went on the stage and became a very competent actor. The Newton Don estate is now the home of the Hon. Mrs Balfour.

Walter entirely approved of what he had done. 'Besides that
we always lived on terms of friendship and intimacy', Scott
wrote to Montagu on Don's death some five years later, 'I
always felt that I owed him much for the candid and liberal
manner in which he interpreted my conduct on an occasion
which may be in your Lordship's recollection . . .'[21] The
fault, it seems, lay with the Sheriff of Roxburghshire,* who
had omitted to name the persons concerned as he had been
directed to do and then made his own mistake an excuse for
excluding them from the Commission. But Scott felt that he
himself should have detected the omission and was honour-
ably prepared to shoulder the blame for the sheriff's short-
comings.** Scott consulted his London solicitor, John Richardson, who replied that Lord Lothian, then in London, was
satisfied that Willie Scott should be a JP for the county and
that he would write to Sir Walter about the other matters on
the morrow.[22] The same day that Scott wrote to Richardson,
he also wrote bitterly to Lothian. 'But really I thought I
might have relied upon his candour and impartiality . . .'
but 'he has acted differently from what I had a title to
expect.'[23] He told Willie that he had had correspondence
both with Don and Richardson about the omitted voters and
that Sir Alexander has forwarded a signed list of their names
to be disposed of at Lord Lothian's pleasure. 'I have written
a long letter to Lord Lothian on the subject and so has Harden.
I trust his Lordship will see it in its true light as an act of
justice to these gentlemen out of which they have [been] cut
short by the Sheriff's conduct.'[24] Lothian was as good as his
word: he wrote to Scott on the morrow of John Richardson's
letter. Furthermore, he did see the matter in its true light.[25]
The omission was rectified forthwith and without further ado.

But if these comparatively trivial matters disconcerted
Scott, he was highly indignant when he discovered the shabby

---

* William Oliver of Dinlabyre, who assumed the additional name
of Rutherford when he succeeded to Edgerston in 1834.
** Why Sir Walter Scott, whose county was Selkirkshire, should
feel himself responsible for the Sheriff of Roxburghshire is not clear.

trick that Robson had played during the election. He had, it seems, written to Nicol Milne of Faldonside, Scott's neighbour and friend, transcribing in full a letter from Lord Montagu promising his support, but omitting to point out that the letter referred to a past election and not to the recent one.[26] Scott wrote about a week later to Montagu

> . . . Now though I thought it impossible but what Mr Robson must have been fully aware of your Lordship's intentions (as you mentioned having written to him) to reserve yourself entirely disengaged and altho' I considered his conduct as not by any means according to Hoyle* yet I had sincere reluctance again to trouble your Lordship on a most unpleasant subject and I will add I was the more loth to do so . . . because I did not like to use the intimacy of your freindly correspondence in a way prejudicial to a poor man who was doing the best he could for his family even although the interest of my own near relation lay opposite. But the inclosed letter from Harden seems to shew that this sort of misrepresentation I can give it no milder name is systematically persisted in and I am therefore reluctantly obliged to place it under your Lordships observation hoping you will put a stop to Mr Robson using your former assurances of support as if they applied to the present canvass. I am sure he does not take the way to serve himself by this species of manoeuvring.'

The whole matter was most dishonest and nothing but 'a catch attempted by the Sheriff. But what says the old song

> *The Maultman** he is cunning*
> *But I can be as slee*
> *And he may crack of his winning*
> *When he clears scores with me.*

I wish to God this matter could be settled amicably . . .'[27]

---

* Edmund Hoyle (1672–1769) whose laws of whist for some years ruled the game.
** A person who stammers, but in Scotland sometimes used to mean a sullen visage or a brawling temper.

To Sir Walter's outburst Lord Montagu advised caution. 'I shall certainly not mention Robsons conduct to any one,' Scott replied, 'though I fancy Maxpopple has been in self-defence contradicting his assertion that he is at present secure of your powerful support. I have no wish to augment the *disagreeables* of this most disagreeable contest . . .'[28] To this Montagu replied disconcertingly that he did not wish to investigate the matter further because exactly similar complaints had reached him that William Scott had represented that he had the Buccleuch interest. 'Now I can perfectly understand the whole case', he wrote pacifically, 'as we have not declared for either party, both naturally express their *expectations* of being supported much more strongly than my Letters at all warrant, these statements after passing through two or three months become positive assertions that each has the Buccleuch Interest.'[29] This nettled Scott. 'Respecting my cousin', he replied, 'I believe him perfectly incapable of representing your Lordship's intentions otherwise than you have stated them to be and if he had by my misapprehension held out his hopes of attaining your patronage before viewing a definite explanation he would I hope have held it the part of an honest man as well as a gentleman to retract any such statement so soon as learned what your Lordship's determination actually was.'[30] In spite of all that Scott could say on his cousin's behalf the Buccleuch family decided to support Robson at next year's election. 'This determination I have by this Post communicated to Scott and Robson', wrote Lord Montagu. 'You know as well as we do all the difficulties we have had to contend with, and you and I have already so fully explained ourselves on this subject that it is quite unnecessary for me to say a word more upon it . . .'[31] Scott told Willie he had learnt this 'very disagreeable information' from his friend Montagu.* But though doubtless chagrined, he must put a good face on it

---

* Sir Walter Scott, Chiefswood, Thursday [September 6, 1821] Maxpoffle, to William Scott, NLS MS 2889, f. 200. Chiefswood is now the home of Professor and Lady Alexandra Trevor-Roper.

. . . I am sure you have followed the line you thought most for the Dukes interest in supporting Mr Robsons interest in this county and tho' I still think neutrality would have better served your purpose I will readily allow that an interested person is no fair judge . . . I willingly take leave of this irksome subject which I hope I have never pressd unduly before your Lordship. At least I am sure I never have and never will trouble you with subjects of complaint which have occurd in the course of the contest although they are of a singular nature and such as I cannot easily forget.[32]

Amidst all this hullabaloo, Willie's finances were not improving, and his miserly father was showing no signs of relenting. So the son was at last reluctantly forced to contemplate selling his home. Sir Walter promised his help. 'If I can hear of a purchaser for Maxpopple I will not fail to recommend it. But,' he added sadly, 'few people are less in the way of knowing folks who may have money to lay out for a residence.'[33] And then a few months later Scott had a bright idea. William Pitt's Income Tax in 1799 to finance the war with France had been dropped in 1802 and a new Income Tax had been introduced in the following year. This new tax had in turn been dropped in 1815. Might it not be revived now? If so why should not his hard-pressed cousin become the Collector in Roxburghshire? 'The only answer to this', he added 'is the uncertainty of the Income Tax being laid on and to this I have really no reply.'[34] In fact there was no revival of this tax until it was reimposed in 1842 by Sir Robert Peel.

Meanwhile, poor Willie was getting more and more discouraged, and—it must be admitted—impatient with his famous cousin who in fact was making every effort on his behalf. 'Nothing gives me more pain in these very unpleasing matters', wrote Walter, 'than that you should think I have some power to serve you which I am not willing to exercise. I assure you it is not so. The difficulty of providing for a person who has no professional claims or views is so great as

to amount almost to impossibility . . .' Willie, it seems, anxious
to take advantage of his cousin's influence, was pressing him
to approach his powerful friends and acquaintances on his
behalf. But Sir Walter would have none of that. 'The *only* and
most unavailing answer I could get from the Duke of Wellington, Lord Mellville* or any other great man wd. be that
nothing occurd to them at present but if any suitable occasion
should offer they would be happy to serve my friend. You
see I cannot get from Lord Mellville, my old and intimate
friend, even a clerks place in the custom house for our cousin
James though promised me over and over. As for the Duke
of W. I am on civil terms with him but by no means such as to
intitle me to ask him for my relatives . . . I hope therefore
you will not be angry with me or think me cold in your interest
for not intruding upon people with requests which it would be
misbecoming in me to make and which must therefore if
made be totally useless to you . . .'[35] Clearly the somewhat
spineless Willie was expecting too much, and we may detect
in this a note of impatience from the kindly Sir Walter, who
perhaps felt in his heart that his cousin might do rather more
to help himself!

But if this was so the mood soon passed, and amidst his
many distractions Sir Walter continued his efforts to help his
tiresome relative.

The reader will recall Collector Rutherford's pacific letter
to Sir Walter Scott the previous summer expressing the hope
that the contest, if continued, might be with 'liberality and
good humour on both sides'. Now at last he showed himself
as good as his word. In April 1822 he and Scott mutually
agreed to an arrangement which would, they hoped, avoid
further unpleasantness. The plan was that Willie Scott should
withdraw from the contest for the collectorship, and in return

---

* Robert Saunders Dundas, second Viscount Melville (1771–1851),
First Lord of the Admiralty since 1812.

Scott and Rutherford would join forces in an effort to prevail upon Montagu and the Buccleuch family to throw the whole of their powerful influence into recommending Willie for the first suitable situation which should become vacant; and they wrote a joint letter to Lord Montagu to that effect.[36] The reply was favourable. 'I was made happy this morning by the assurance that the Convention of Jedburgh meets with your Lordship's approbation . . .' wrote Scott. Thus the heat was taken out of the affair. 'Mr Rutherford wrote me a very kind letter on the subject expressing his satisfaction that freinds would be freinds and cousins cousins once more. I have also Harden's approbation: in short all will be pleased except those who have an interest in wishing a schism between the freinds of the Buccleuch interest . . .'[37]. Of course this was a partial retreat, but a retreat from a position that must have been lost. 'Maxpopple has given up his competition for the Collector-ship which he must have lost,' Scott admitted to his son Walter, 'I manoeuvred for him so as to gain a positive promise from Lord Montagu . . . that he shall have an equivalent provision when such is open and yet I doubt if he thanks me for substituting an excellent chance for a bad one though it is the same as if I had given him a sound horse for a lame one. I never had so much plague with an individual as with this wrong headed man and yet he is an honourable kind hearted fellow at bottom and his large family require assistance much . . .'[38] And later that year to Willie's brother Hugh. 'We have had a smart contest on his behalf since you went away and were at last driven to a compromise which however I have good hopes will produce some advantage to him. Your excellent Mother enjoys such health as can be expected at her advanced state of life—all other freinds much as usual . . .'[39] 'Maxie is here duller than ditchwater and prosy to a horror about India and Penang', he told his son Walter, at Dresden, 'I have given him an old Indian Register while I scrible these few lines . . .'[40]

So ended in disappointment Willie Scott's hopes of becoming Collector of Cess for the County of Roxburgh.

CHAPTER THREE

Sir Walter Scott—the last years

IN SPITE of Willie Scott's moody temper and ingratitude his famous and very busy cousin continued to do all he could to help him obtain employment in his county. 'There is only one situation in Roxburgh which would suit and it is beset with difficulties of a very peculiar kind, but which I think might be got over were the place vacant.' This was probably the Distributorship of Stamps, held by John Riddel. If that surmise is correct, the place was not vacant. For a post in another county Willie would have to contemplate moving house, which would presumably mean selling Maxpoffle; much to be regretted but unavoidable in the circumstances.[1] Walter hoped to be back at Abbotsford on February 14 and see his cousin, but that meeting had to be cancelled. He then proposed a meeting after March 12 when 'We shall then I think see daylight through our business and at least know whether we must go on another tack or no.'[2] We do not know if this meeting took place; what we do know is that some weeks later Willie was asking his cousin for a loan to buy feus in order to give himself income. But Sir Walter's finances were being stretched to the uttermost by the cost of the completion and decoration of Abbotsford. 'I would be glad to assist you in any thing in my power', he told Willie, 'but my cash is too low considering the expence of building here etc. to be of any service in the matter of Feus. I should be also afraid that such a transaction however desirable in other respects would be attended with much expence for should Maxpopple not sell you would have to insure your life for the price against your father's, that is to say insure for a sum payable upon your own demise if you should predecease him', all of which would be very expensive.'³ A part of 'the expense of building here' was making bricks for the enormous walls round the fruit garden at Abbotsford, and Scott showed his continued kindness to his cousin in offering free of charge as many bricks as Willie could do with. Furthermore some six weeks later he demonstrated his generosity further by lending Willie £140 'belonging to a small trust which is in my person'.⁴

As the year wore on Walter Scott was forced to admit to his cousin that they were making no progress—presumably in the matter of the Distributorship of Stamps. 'I have only the satisfaction to think that I have done all that was possible to advance what would have been an arrangement agreeable to you.'⁵ Not much comfort to poor Willie who proceeded to indulge in an orgy of self-pity. Poor feeble man, ever seeking to take advantage of his cousin's fame: he seems a rather pathetic piece of flotsam on the world's boisterous sea.

By the end of the year 1824, Abbotsford was nearing completion. So at Christmas Sir Walter and Lady Scott entertained a large party. On January 7, they gave a ball thus described by one of the guests in his journal.

> To-day my sister Fanny and I came here [Abbotsford]. In the evening there was a dance in honour of Sir Walter Scott's eldest son, who had recently come from Sandhurst College, after having passed through some military examinations with great credit. We had a great clan of Scotts. There were others besides from the neighbourhood—at least half-a-dozen Fergusons, with the jolly Sir Adam at their head—Lady Ferguson, her niece Miss Jobson, the pretty heiress of Lochore. The evening passed very merrily, with much spirited dancing; and the supper was extremely cheerful and quite superior to that of Hogmanay.'⁶

No wonder it was a cheerful evening for the Scotts' elder son, Walter, had become engaged to 'the pretty heiress of Lochore'

—a 'very sweet little girl', Sir Walter told Willie,*

> a niece of Lady Ferguson. Her father William Jobson of Lochore in Fifeshire was a merchant in London. . . . Her mother was one of the Stuarts of Stenhouse [*sic* for Stenton]. The fortune is very considerable being rather above than under £50,000—the only burthen her mother's jointure of £500 per annum. So Abbotsford will stand pretty fast so far as cash is concerned. The favour of the public has enabled me to make very good settlements with little temporary inconvenience. It is uncertain where or when the wedding will take place—if in the country I hope you will attend . . . I will let you know about our arrangements when completely settled.'[7]

The marriage between young Walter Scott and Jane Jobson took place in Edinburgh on February 3. We do not know whether Raeburn and his wife from Lessudden attended; we may be sure that their son and his wife from Maxpoffle were present at all the festivities. We can also be sure that Willie's enjoyment of all these family jollifications was vastly enhanced by some wonderful news that his cousin was able to give him.

On January 26—little more than a week before the wedding —Scott's Sheriff-Substitute of Selkirk, Charles Erskine ninth of Shielfield, suffered an apoplectic fit in Jedburgh, which rapidly proved fatal. Now the position of Sheriff-Substitute, thus so unexpectedly vacated, was in the gift of the Sheriff-Depute of the County, Scott himself. He knew, of course, that his unfortunate cousin would be quick to beg him to bestow the office on him, so he had to act smartly, as he explained to Lord Montagu. '. . . Poor Maxpopple failed not to be a candidate *cum plurimis aliis*. I should have been

---

* 'She is low of stature', he told his friend Morritt, 'which is not amiss Walter being as you know Patagonian—has no pretensions to beauty but is what may be fairly called pretty and as she has fine legs and regular features she looks at time extremely interesting.' Scott, n.d. [PM, March 25, 1825] to Morritt, 24 Steign, Brighton. Scott, *Letters*, IX, 22–3.

ruined by postage had I not come to an immediate decision. I suppose the first directions I had to give to Maxie he would be for calling me out for not treating him with due ceremony.'[8] But though Walter Scott was truly anxious to help Willie, the long and faithful services of Andrew Lang as Sheriff and Commissary Clerk and Clerk of the Peace for Selkirkshire* could not be overlooked. The vacant post must first be offered to him. But Sir Walter attached a condition to the offer that made it likely that Lang would refuse: he must no longer meddle in Burgh politics. As Scott anticipated Lang declined the appointment. 'In these circumstances and Andrew Lang having undertaken to drynurse him for a year or two I shall not hesitate to give Maxpopple the office[9] as spite of his confounded pride he is intelligent and honest and well acquainted with country business. Thus a plaguy load will be taken off my mind and some trouble my dear Lord spared to you . . .'[10] And to Willie's brother, Hugh, he wrote 'You will have heard that the death of poor Charles Erskine has enabled me to make your brother William rather better by a new office of about £260 which in his unlucky circumstances and with a spirit above his means will always be of some service.'[11]

This appointment was perhaps the most important event in Willie's life and he was filled with excitement. 'The moans of Maxpopple are indeed silenced for the present. He came to Abbotsford when I had some Mertoun folks and Sir Adam with his Lady and thus so far laid aside his dignity as a Hidalgo that he danced drank and sang Blue bonnets over the border together with that emphatic ditty of which the burthen runs—

Let the cymbals clang with a merry merry bang

So obstreperous was he in his mirth that my little daughter seemd to think that she had become allied to the "dancing

---

* He was grandfather of Andrew Lang (1844–1912), scholar, poet and man of letters.

Fawn".'[12] Yet even in his gratitude Willie was still hoping for better things to follow. 'For this Act of charity conferred on me and mine we now make our humble acknowledgements', he wrote, adding: 'But before I close it occurs to me to say that I shall if you please relinquish this Substituteship when we succeed in the County for the situation we have in view.'[13]

Splendid as was the post to which Walter had just appointed his cousin it had for Willie one considerable disadvantage: the appointment was as Sheriff-Substitute for Selkirkshire, and the Sheriff-Substitute was required to reside in his own county. Willie feared that he would be forced to dispose of Maxpoffle; and with that in view Sir Walter had actually recommended it to Lord Craigie, a Scottish judge who was looking for a house. 'But the learned Judge chuses a house ready furnished', he told Willie 'which of course renders him out of the question.'[14] To the proposition that he should move into Selkirkshire Willie offered the strongest resistance; and it seems clear that he wrote to Cousin Walter bitterly complaining that it was grossly unfair that the Sheriff-Depute of Selkirkshire should be allowed to live in Roxburghshire whilst his Substitute had to dig up his roots and move across the county border. This caused Sir Walter to lose his temper. 'Neither King nor Exchequer have any thing to do with my residence', he told Willie for once angered by his ungrateful relative; yet he gave Willie some useful hints as to how he might qualify by having certified lodgings in Selkirkshire and still retain Maxpoffle. Indeed, there seems no end to the wonderful good-nature of the one cousin and the crass stupidity of the other!

Yet it must be admitted that Willie had a due sense of responsibility in his new post. According to his cousin he attended well to the work of his sheriffdom; and, in spite of much grumbling, he found himself a residence in Selkirkshire.[15] Furthermore, he longed to be able to repay the money Walter Scott had lent him. 'When the time comes I shall instanta free myself from all such obligations,' he assured him. 'My crime is poverty. I hope not want of honour, and many a good man in my situation has felt that evil, which all my great interest of 5 years ago was not able to ease me of, and were it not for the situation I hold under you and [for] which I am solely indebted to you I might go into durance vile. But I have lasted long in hope and trust to weather the storm.'[16] And a month later he wrote feelingly of his patron's financial reverses. 'If you are blessed with good health and live as some of your ancestors, I still hope you may get free of all and every encumbrance, unless the deficit proves heavier than I can possibly imagine. I am also sure that you have many friends and well wishers for your future happiness in this world, independent of your blood relations, which is a pleasing consideration.'[17]

Whilst all this was afoot kindly Robert in Penang, seeing his hard pressed brother's family constantly increasing, sent him a gift of £300. 'I see you have got another addition to your family—there is certainly an abundant supply of the Raeburn family now and there is I think but little chance of a lack of an heir for the Estate for some considerable time to come . . .' In fact the line did not fail until nearly a century and a half later. '. . . the laird I see has let the fields round the house for a long period—he must be getting very rich . . .'[18] At first he did not much like the idea of Willie moving house. 'I must acknowledge I could wish you to remain near to the Old Folks at Lessudden House and offer them all the little comfort that you can in their old days', he told his brother a few months later. At the same time he showed Willie that the future was not unpromising. 'It is needless to say any thing regarding the Laird and his money matters: we all know it has ever been the same . . . and as for expecting that he would ever reconcile himself to becoming more liberal as he advanced in age it is totally out of the question, but . . . as he does not expend any money there will be the more left for you by and by. I feel for the uncomfortable situation that you are often placed in but cannot exactly see how the thing is at present to be remedied . . .'[19] But when Willie wrote to his brother complaining of the need for him to move into Selkirkshire where he had been forced to take a small cottage, Robert replied sympathetically that it was a pity he could not transport his own house over the county border. But the sacrifice must be made. 'The Depute Sheriffship [Sheriff-Substitute-ship] as you say is too good a thing to let slip in any quarter of the world—indeed [in] times as the present, it is a comfortable thing to have to look to. . . .'[20]

The happiness that Sir Walter Scott derived from his elder son's marriage was soon turned to sorrow. His wife was obviously dying and on May 1, 1826 Barbara Scott of Raeburn walked over from Lessudden to see the invalid. 'I think she was shocked with the melancholy change', recorded the sorrowing husband. But he had the presence of mind to order the carriage to take his cousin home. She however would have none of it and insisted on walking back to Lessudden House 'making her walk 16 or 18 miles'.[21] Just over a fortnight later, on May 16, 1826, Lady Scott died at Abbotsford. Scott's son Walter was with his regiment and the unhappy father turned for comfort to his younger boy, then at Oxford. Willie had tried to play his part but could not fill the breach. 'Indeed I have no nearer friend to assist me than Maxpopple' he told Charles, 'whose good meaning is provokingly chequered with folly, and there is much to be arranged.'[22] He also turned to his niece Anne, Tom Scott's daughter, 'a prudent, sensible and kindly young woman,' who hastened from Cheltenham.[23] A week later they buried her in the grounds of Dryburgh Abbey, where her husband was to join her some seven years later.

It was not long before poor Scott had once more to cope with the crass stupidity of his tiresome cousin. Sir Walter's lifelong friend, John Wilson Croker*, Secretary of the Admiralty, and Sir George Cockburn**, the admiral, MP for Plymouth

---

* John Wilson Croker (1780–1857), politician and essayist.
** Sir George Cockburn (1772–1853), Admiral of the Fleet.

and a junior lord of the Admiralty, had, it seems, been exerting their considerable influence on Willie's behalf only to receive from that awkward customer a rude—not to say offensive—letter. Croker, not unnaturally looking for thanks, not abuse, though the kindest and mildest of men wrote angrily to Scott. Sir Walter was exasperated, yet even in his anger he continued to find some excuses for Willie's folly. 'My dear Croker', he wrote,

> you cannot surely suppose me the accessory to the folly of Maxpopple (W. Scott videlicet) which has given me the most sincere uneasiness. I forwarded your letter to him and receiving an answer in the tone of that which he was so ill-advised as to send you I replied that I washed my hands of all such negotiations which I considered as entirely out of place and season and should expect him to tell me in two words whether he meant thankfully to accept the great favour as offered as otherwise I would understand him to decline it and write to Sir George Cockburn and you to give yourselves no more trouble in the matter. Other of his friends had given him the same advice and I got a letter from him yesterday stating that he was to be guided by it. I have little to say in excuse of Maxie's conduct except that he is a sort of original which exists here and there in Scotland, a good gentleman-like honorable man in all his feelings, but beset with the two great national evils Pride and Poverty. He is a Scottish Hidalgo with a high sense of his own hereditary consequence, an idea that all the world must or ought to be occupied in attending to the fate of himself and his family with a slight occasional suspicion that this is not the case so much as it ought to [be]. He has never been able exactly to understand how I came to become a baronet being only a cadet of his family. [One wonders if even Willie Scott of Raeburn can have been quite as absurd as that!] In short he is a great quizz. But then he has a wife and twelve children and what is worse an old papa who unnaturally persists in foxhunting though upwards of 80 and will not vacate possession of the family estate. So Maxpopple must really be forgiven by

Sir George Cockburn and you and as to what part of your kindness has not been duly acknowledged allow me to make it up by my sense that the utmost has been done in the kindest and handsomest manner and that I am on my Cousin's account as well as my own, very much your obliged and thankful Walter Scott.'[24]

How utterly absurd Willie Scott could be—absurd and exasperating! So, is it fanciful to suppose that, when a few years later Sir Walter was painting the portrait of Godfrey Bertram the futile laird of Ellangowan, he may have had his cousin in mind? True, in one respect they vastly differed, for Scott had twelve children, whereas Bertram had but two: but that was necessary to the story, for the loss of an heir with eleven brothers and sisters to comfort a sorrowing parent is not half so poignant as the loss of the heir, leaving but one motherless daughter to the poor laird. In other respects the lairds of Raeburn and Ellangowan seem remarkably alike. Their pride in their ancestry, their poverty, their feckless disregard of finance, their lack of energy, their preoccupation with trifles, their reliance on others to help them—'Without a single spark of energy to meet or repel these misfortunes', we are told, 'Godfrey put his faith in the activity of another' under whose supervision 'small debts grew into large, interest were accumulated upon capitals, movable bonds became heritable, and law charges were heaped upon all . . .'[25]— their anxiety to obtain employment in the county—'No sir,' Godfrey tells Mannering impatiently, 'the name of Godfrey Bertram of Ellangowan is *not* in the last commission, though there's scarce a carle in the county that has a ploughgate of land, but what he must write to quarter-sessions and write JP after his name':[26] all this suggests a singular likeness between the two lairds. There is no certainty of course, but it does look as if Godfrey Bertram of Ellangowan may be a satirical portrait of William Scott of Raeburn.

The year 1828 was a sad one for both the cousins. In July Willie lost his eldest son Walter, drowned in HMS *Acorn*. He was only seventeen. 'I had hardly parted from poor Hector Macdonald', Sir Walter told his son-in-law, 'when I had to visit Maxpopple whose eldest son is on board the unfortunate *Acorn* and Brewster whose 2nd boy was drowned in Tweed the other day. It is most dismal work.'[27] At the same time Willie's aged mother was nearing her end. Sir Walter had always had a soft spot in his heart for his aunt—'Lady Raeburn' as he invariably called her—in spite of his hostile feelings towards his uncle. 'We left Mertoun after breakfast, and the two Annes* and I visited Lady Raeburn at Lessudden', he had noted in his Journal a few years previously. 'My Aunt is now in her ninetieth year—so clean, so nice, so well arranged in every respect, that it makes old age lovely. She talks both of later and former events with perfect possession of her faculties, and has only failed in her limbs. A great deal of kind feeling has survived, in spite of the frost of years.'[28] And now the nonagenarian Jean Scott of Raeburn was dying. 'I am sorry for my poor Aunt', wrote Sir Walter to Willie two days after her death;[29] and he wrote sadly to his daughter Sophia: 'Our worthy old Aunt Lady Raeburn, is gone,' he wrote, 'and I am now the eldest living person of my father's family.'[30] 'The death of our Revered Mother', wrote Robert to his brother, 'is a truly sorrowful event but still we must, and ought, to be truly thankful to God for his great goodness in having permitted her to sojourn among us here below, for such a lengthened period, indeed latterly her sufferings and distress were, I understood, so great that a long prolongation of her life was not to be wished for—to all of us she has ever been a most kind, warm hearted and truly affectionate Mother, and her many virtues will I am confident be cherished by all her children to the last hour of this existence. . . .'[31]

When her husband followed her to the grave a year later,

---

* Sir Walter's younger daughter and Anne his brother Tom's daughter.

there were no such lamentations from any of his children. The notice inserted in the *Kelso Mail* on Monday, November 3, was composed by Sir Walter: 'Died at Lessudden on the 20th October in the ninety second year of her age Mrs Jean Scott, wife of Walter Scott Esquire of Raeburn. She retained possession of her faculties at this advanced period of human life and will be long regretted by her relatives and friends and by the poor to whom she was a liberal benefactress.'* A worthy epitaph.

Six months later died another old friend of the family, the crack-brained Earl of Buchan, 'the silliest and vainest of busy-bodies', as Lockhart called him.[32] 'Lord Buchan is dead', Scott recorded in his Journal for April 20, 'a person whose immense vanity, bordering upon insanity, obscured, or rather eclipsed, very considerable talents. His imagination was so fertile, that he seemed really to believe the extraordinary fictions which he delighted in telling . . .'[33] On one occasion he had the effrontery, it seems, to give to Robert Burns 'unsolicited bad advice' on how to write poetry.[34] He raised immense and tasteless memorials to the poet Thomson and to Sir William Wallace. And back in 1819 when Walter Scott was suffering his very serious illness in Castle Street and was thought to be *in extremis,* this well-meaning but absurd man tried to force an entrance into the house to tell the family of the elaborate arrangements he had in contemplation for Sir Walter's funeral, which included an eulogy to be pronounced by him over the grave, after the fashion of French Academicians in the *Père La Chaise.*[35]

What a fate Sir Walter had missed; and now he and Cousin Willie were setting out to attend the poor old man's funeral in the family chapel among the ruins of Dryburgh Abbey. And even on this solemn occasion there was something odd, something unusual. The body was in the grave, but with the

* The copy of the notice now in the National Library of Scotland is endorsed in William Scott's hand. 'Announcement of the death of my Mother written by her nephew, Sir Walter.' NLS MS 2890, f. 78.

feet pointing westward. Cousin Willie suggested that they should take notice of this, 'but I assured him that a man who had been wrong in the head all his life would scarce become right-headed after death'. Then he had some melancholy reflections. It was his first visit to the ruins since his wife's funeral. 'My next visit may be involuntary. Even so God's will be done. At least I have not the mortification of thinking what a deal of patronage and fuss Lord Buchan would bestow on my funeral.' Willie Scott and four of his family returned to Abbotsford to dine and sleep, and the young people were no doubt amused at what they heard of the day's events at Dryburgh.[36]

Raeburn did not long survive his wife, though he was in fact some years her junior. He died in the summer of 1830. Sir Walter pretended no regrets. 'My dear Cousin', he wrote to Willie, 'I learn'd by your letter this morning the departure of my uncle and felt as we must all do at the removal of an ancient landmark. My regard for the family of my Aunt and many other circumstances will most certainly lead me to attend the funeral on Monday and I will come to Abbotsford on Saturday night or Monday with that purpose . . .'[37] In his Journal Sir Walter was more outspoken.

> I came here [Abbotsford] to attend Raeburn's funeral. I am near of his kin, my great grandfather, Walter Scott, being the second son or first cadet of this small family. My late kinsman was also married to my aunt, a most amiable old lady. He was never kind to me, and at last utterly ungracious. Of course I never liked him, and we kept no terms. He had forgot, though, an infantine cause of quarrell, which I always rememberd. When I was four or five years old I was staying at Lessudden House, an old mansion, the abode of this Raeburn. A large pigeon house was almost destroyd with Starlings, then a common bird, though now seldom seen. They were seized in their nests and put in a bag, and I think drowned, or threshed to death, or put to some such end. The servants gave one to me, which I in some degree tamed, and the brute of a laird seized and rung its [neck.] I flew at his throat like a wild cat, and was torn from

him with no little difficulty. Long afterwards I did him
the mortal offence to recall some superiority which my
father had lent to the laird to make up a qualification,
which he meant to exercise by voting for Lord Minto's
interest against poor Don. This made a total breach
between two relations who had never been friends, and
though I was afterwards of considerable service to his
family, he kept his ill-humour, alleging justly enough
that I did these kind actions for the sake of his wife and
family, not for his benefit. I now saw him at the age of
eighty-two or three deposited in the ancestral grave,
dined with my cousins, and returned to Abbotsford
about eight o'clock.[38]

Meanwhile good-natured Robert in far away Penang
watched events at home, and hearing that his nephew Alexander,* now a lad of sixteen, was to go to college, sent his
brother £100 'to help to pay Alexander's expenses in Edinburgh'.[39] In point of fact Robert was on the point of sailing
for Britain and not very long afterwards we find him visiting
his brother Hugh at Draycott. 'We intend leaving here
tomorrow morning', he wrote to Willie on mourning paper
for his parents, 'and as the weather I think should become
better I shall take a look at Liverpool . . .'[40] on his way to
Lessudden as the new laird's guest. On July 15 Scott visited
Lessudden and two days later there was a family dinner
party there. 'A dinner of Cousins, the young Laird of Raeburn . . .
his brother Robert, who has been in India for forty years,
excepting one short visit: a fine manly fellow, who has belled
the cat with fortune, and held her at bay as a man of mould
may. Being all kinsmen and friends, we made a merry day of
our re-union.'[41]

Now that Willie had become Raeburn he was anxious to
dispose of Maxpoffle, but this apparently gave him some
trouble. 'I am glad to notice', wrote Robert from Perth two
months later, 'that you have at last got Maxpoffle off your
hands. . . .'[42] He sold the property which he had considerably

---

* Willie's eldest son since the loss of Walter in HMS *Acorn* in 1828.

enlarged during his twenty-three years of ownership, to John Ainslie, eldest son of Colonel John Ainslie of Teviotgrove for £5,750.*

For the first few months after his return to England Robert had constantly changed his residence from place to place. But he soon tired of this and decided to spend the winter at Mackenzie's Hotel in Edinburgh until he could move into a

---

* The Disposition is dated November 16, 1830 and registered in the Books of Council and Session on June 26, 1833. It must also have been recorded in the Register of Sasines, which applies to all documents dealing with lands. I am grateful to Mr Francis Stewart, ws, for this information.

The subjects are set out as follows:

1) ALL and WHOLE five merkland of Maxpoffle comprehending the feuduties and superiorities of those parts formerly belonging in property to John Duncanson and Thomas Stenhouse so far as feus did not belong in property to William Scott; Also right of property in those parts of the feus acquired from the Trustees for Alexander Chatto of Mainhouse and Others; Together with the farm and lands of Westquarter formerly possessed by Thomas Stenhouse (excepting (1) part of said lands lying on south side of the public drove road leading towards St Boswells Green adjoining the lands of Camieston sold to the Trustees for William Riddell of Camieston in 1817 and (2) part of field called Woodpark which (since its intersection by the new road leading from St Boswells Green to Selkirk) now lies on the south side of the same, consisting of 6½ acres English measure excambed with the Trustee for William Riddell for 4⅓ acres English measure on the north side of the road).

2) ALL and WHOLE the lands and others (particularly described) in the south crofts of Bowden.

3) ALL and WHOLE these four rigs or buts of land in crofts on south side of Bowden (also particularly described).

4) ALL and WHOLE the Nether Mill of Bowden, kiln and houses thereto belonging, together with the Mill lands lately possessed by William Swanston.

5) ALL and WHOLE the said 4⅓ acres (whereof 1.6 acres described as young plantations) bounded on south and west by the new turnpike road, on the north by the old drove road, and on the east by the angle of the lands of Maxpoffle near the spot where the different lines of the road separate.

house he had leased for six months, No. 25 Abercromby Place, 'The situation is good', he told William, 'but the terms I think high, but it is as well to have done, as I am not fond of ranging about for houses . . . I do not think that I shall leave Town again, and as soon as I have got the House ready I shall write Barbara to come . . . .'[43] A few weeks later came word of the death of Robert's eldest son, Harry, in Penang. The sad news came by his second son Charles.[44] 'My dear Robert', wrote Willie to his sorrowing brother, 'Before leaving Selkirk today I received with surprise and grief your letter of yesterday—poor Harry, his career has been short indeed and I lament his loss and lament *your* loss, knowing well from several trials that all other distresses are trifles compared with the loss of children . . .'[45] Amidst these unhappy distractions Robert wrote to tell his brother '*I am quite ready for your reception whenever you may choose to come in* and as Alexander is to be placed at School on the 1st November you had better bring him with you, and we will take care of him for the winter . . .'[46] So Alexander was left for the next few months under the care of his Uncle Robert and Aunt Barbara, who had availed herself of Robert's offer to give her a home in Edinburgh.

But even now after old Raeburn's death it does not appear as if Willie's finances were any too easy. He was anxious to purchase from his late father's trustees some of the land belonging to the estate. 'I readily admit that your wish is a natural one enough to retain if possible as much of the old Family Estate as you can', wrote Robert, but is he, he asked, in a position to do this without embarrassing himself? As for Robert, he did not want any say in the winding up of the estate, having already renounced to his sister Barbara any rights he might have under the Will. 'This being the case I have not, nor do I wish to have, the slightest influence whatever in any of the arrangements regarding the estate that are to be carried into effect according to the terms of the Will.' Furthermore, Willie had offered Robert the use of Lessudden House 'for summer quarters . . . but my movements are quite uncertain, and therefore I beg you will not consider me at all in the matter . . .'[47]

Whilst Alexander stayed with his uncle and aunt in Edinburgh, his father gave him little commissions, such as matching up some wall paper. 'I have got this paper, which is the likest [sic] to the piece that you sent . . . All the difference is that the one has got a red flour [sic] and the other a white, but I showed it to Uncle Robert and he thinks that it will do— he thinks that nobody will ever notice it . . .'[48] Alexander was now eighteen, and uncertainties as to his future were causing both his father and his uncle anxiety. Thus Robert wrote to his brother to say that he had not as yet spoken to the boy about his future, adding ominously, '. . . I must confess the prospect of his being able to do any thing for himself appears distant . . . I fear he will not have benefited much by his attendance at College this winter, as it appears that few of the scholars are ever asked a question of any kind . . .'[49] Yet he had not been idle. The question was whether he should go in for the law and become a ws or buy a commission in the army. There were difficulties in either course. The boy had seen a General Stewart who said he was an old friend of his father's in days gone by but that it was long since they had met. He regretted that he could not help, having tried for the son of a very old friend killed in battle to be allowed to buy a commission but to no effect. He advised Alexander to make application to the Duke of Buccleuch who 'will have more interest since the change of Ministers' and his father to write to Lord Montagu.[50]

At about this time Willie's younger brother John, a Major in the Bengal N.C., who had long suffered from that most distressing complaint asthma, and who, after making a small fortune in the East Indies, had settled at a little house he built near Melrose, which he called Ravenswood, decided to leave for Jamaica. Sir Walter parted with him with some regret. 'Without having been intimate friends', he recorded, 'we were always affectionate relations, and now we part, probably never to meet in this world. He has a good deal of the character said to belong to the family. Our parting with mutual feeling may be easily supposed.'[51] The cousins probably never met again, for the major died in June 1832.

Meanwhile, Alexander continued attendance at college throughout the winter in the hopes of one day becoming a lawyer. But life was full of difficulties for the poor boy. First, he lost his purse with £4 in it; secondly he did not like to take out a ticket for the Latin class before hearing from his father, though Latin was a necessary subject for an aspiring lawyer. His hesitation was due to the fact that the profession was then much overcrowded and that there was every chance that even if he went on and served his apprenticeship he might be thrown out. Furthermore, his tutor Cleghorn was not encouraging. 'Aunt Barbara says that Mr Cleghorn said . . . that unless I was very clever, diligent, and industrious that I had not the least chance to succeed as a writer to the signet. Uncle Robert says that there are many young men who are very clever and have as good chances as me, and who are ready to commence business and can't get any. . . . Now, my dear Father, I wish you could consider this, and let me know as soon as possible what is to be done for at present I am quite at a stand.'[52] Meanwhile, Robert wrote to his brother questioning whether it would be wise for Alexander to continue his studies this winter for 'a very heavy outlay' is needed 'to set a young person agoing and also to support him during his apprenticeship of 5 years &c &c—and after all it is very questionable whether a young man on his own bottom would be able to find employment sufficient to support himself . . .'[53] But whatever Mr Cleghorn told Aunt Barbara, after talking things over with Uncle Robert he agreed to take Alexander into his office at once; but he must go to college for a further period to attend the 'Logick class' which will only take up one hour a day and Mr Copeland must give him private coaching in Latin. Then he turned to a more genial subject. 'Uncle John arrived here on Sunday from London by steam . . . he came by the Royal William, a passage of six days—they were obliged to put back twice and landed at Berwick.' His Uncle

Robert had made good the £4 lost in his purse; and grandmama has promised to make him a present of 'a great coat which is now in the hands of the Taylor . . .'[54]

Alexander's next letter home dealt with money which was running short, and life at college, he said, was expensive. 'My dear Father', he wrote, 'I write to let you know that the money that you left with Unce [*sic*] Robt. is done and that [I] will need some more if convenient, for we are quite run out, as our Masters get their payment at the beginning of the quarters—and whenever we are asked out to a party, then we have our share of the Coach to pay, which comes rather expensive—but money goes very little way in Edinburgh before we get every little thing pay'd.' This frankly was just not true. A poor student could live in Edinburgh University at that time on a few pounds for fees and a few shillings a week for lodgings. It looks as if Alexander was following in his father's footsteps and was anxious to live in a grander style than his finances warranted.

We have been at two balls, one at Mrs Murray's a Dance Lady, the widow of a Doctor Murray who bought Uncle Hugh's ship, and another at Mrs Cheine's which both lasted till 2 in the morning. Susan[55] is very fond of balls, dinners, and tea drinkings—she dances a great deal at these parties, and is always in a great hurry to get away to them—whenever to a friend's house such as Aunt Charlotte's or Mrs Meeks she never will wait on me, but runs away about an hour before me. I was called up at College on Tuesday the 4th of January for the first time and perhaps the last—by good luck got a sentence that was not very difficult—I never have gone to my drawing master yet, as I have been waiting to hear from you about it—I mentioned it in my letter to Mama but never have heard anything about it. Uncle Robert does not want me to go to any one without being recommended by some person, and I never have been able to see any one who could tell me a word about them—Susan was telling me something about a Miss Andrews who is a beautiful drawer, and teaches Ladies and Gentlemen—

I hope that when you write to me you will say what I have to do, for I am impatient to get some lessons as I have time—I like my writing master Mr Scott very much. I have done a great deal of Arithmetic with him, and gone through the day Book and Ledger. Uncle Robt. got your letter yesterday morning and is to answer it soon. All join with me in sending kind compliments to you all. I am your affect. son Alex. Scott.[56]

'You say you are quite happy that I have made commencement with Mr Cleghorn,' Alexander wrote to his father a fortnight later, 'and so am I for I am making at least 4 or 5 shillings a day which I think is very good pay . . .' Then he turned to a sad subject: the Lockharts' sickly boy had died at last. 'I was very sorry to hear of the death of poor Johnie Lockhart, but indeed it was not to be wished that his life should be prolonged. I dare say he must have suffered a great deal . . .'[57] But if Alexander was contented, his Uncle Robert was still dubious of his continuing his Latin lessons at home and his Logic class at college, for '. . . I believe he receives but little *if any benefit* from the lectures he hears, as yet he has never been called up or asked a single question by the Professor . . .'[58] Furthermore, he thinks that his nephew shows no particular predilection for 'the Writer Trade' and states that he has no objection to a 'Military line of life'. So he begs his father to write and ask Lord Montagu if he will help to procure for him an ensign's commission in the army. 'It is truly a difficult matter to determine', wrote Robert, 'what is best to be done with young men in these times . . .'[59]

But Alexander was growing up and he had a mind of his own. 'I don't know what passed between you and Uncle Robert at Lessudden', he told his father, 'but if you think it impossible to get me into the Army and have given up thought of making me a ws I have only to state that I don't wish to go to India upon any account unless it was to hold a situation of a very superior nature . . .'[60] And a month later, when his uncle suggested that he might go out to Canada if somebody could be found to go with him, he told his father that there was slender chance of making a fortune there.

> I don't doubt that a person going out might make a
> very comfortable livelihood as long as they stayed there,
> but I have got no idea of staying there all my life. What
> I want to do is to make money and if I have to go to a
> foreign land to seek it I go with an expectation of coming
> home to Scotland to spend the latter part of my life with
> it . . . I am in great impatience to be settled at something
> as it looks very awkward when a person asks me what I
> am going to be, and [I am] not able to tell them, and I
> am also now getting up in years and I think the sooner
> it is settled the better . . .[61]

Three weeks later he was on the same theme. 'I should like
to know what are your thoughts or views with regard to what
I am next to turn my hand to,' he told his father with
obviously increased impatience . . . 'I wish I maint stick on
your hands, as situations of every kind are so difficult to be
got in the present time . . .'[62]

Whilst the Sheriff-Substitute of Selkirk was thus worrying
about his son Alexander's future, he was perforce corresponding at length with his superior, the Sheriff-Depute, on various
matters connected with the office; and we have some echoes
of these events. Thus Willie reports to Walter that petty
theft among children is rife in the county, and recommends as
punishment a tread mill, '. . . which I much wish you would
recommend to the attention of the Country Gentlemen and
Magistrates of the Borough'.[63] How the country gentlemen
and magistrates of the borough reacted, history does not
relate. On another occasion he told the Sheriff-Depute that
Mr Thomson and Water Bailiff Graham had had to run for
their lives from a volley of stones and had been forced to take
shelter in a private house. They were rescued by Mr Lang who
was himself struck in the back by a stone. Some twenty
witnesses had been examined but it had not proved possible
to discover who had struck Thomson; but they were confident
that they knew Lang's assailant. Will the Sheriff-Depute
approve the offer of a reward of three or four guineas to

anybody who can give information?[64] And five months later we find the Substitute telling his superior that one Thomas Hewat, who had at the last assizes been ordered to be imprisoned for eighteen months, had been seen riding in the street of Selkirk roaring drunk on the night of the Burgh Election. 'I do think it my duty', wrote Willie, 'to state this to you and to state that I consider Rodger the Jailer an unfit person to have charge of the Prison. . . .'[65] But it is unlikely that Sir Walter was much concerned with his cousin's views, which he certainly did not value; indeed, it is said that so little did he rely on Willie's discrimination that he always insisted on signing the judgments himself and never allowed Raeburn to sign any on his behalf.[66] But the Sheriff-Depute was failing, and on October 29 he sailed from Portsmouth for a milder climate. On November 22 he reached Malta and on December 14th embarked for Naples. Here the distressing news reached him of the death of his grandson, John Hugh Lockhart—his dearly loved 'Hugh Littlejohn'. This was a sad blow. In mid-April he left for Rome, where he insisted on visiting the tomb in St Peter's of the last of the Stewarts. And so in May and June he passed through the Tyrol and sailed down the Rhine. On June 9 at Nimuegen he was seized with an attack of apoplexy and paralysis, and was ordered home. He reached London on July 7 in a semi-conscious state: it was evident that his life was slowly ebbing. 'You will be shocked to hear of the severe illness of my father. There is I fear not the slightest hope of his recovery', reported his son Walter. 'Thank God, he suffers no pain and sinks very gradually.'[67] His great purpose now was to reach his beloved home before he died. On July 7 he left London by steamboat to Newhaven, near Edinburgh, whence he was taken by carriage to Abbotsford. 'Sir Walter had stood his journey well and is to-day better than he has been since he touched England,' his son-in-law, Lockhart, told Willie. Then Lockhart turned to another topic. William Scott was anxious to resign his post as Sheriff-Substitute. Now that he was laird of Raeburn he no longer needed the salary: and Scott's absence abroad, when he had been forced to act unaided, had taught him now inadequate he was for his duties. 'The matter you write about is very important and if you can call here any time tomorrow we must contrive to fix what should be done. Sir Walter can't *sign* anything, observe.'[68] As he could not write he could neither resign his Sheriffdom nor nominate a substitute. The Crown could not appoint a new depute so long as the depute was alive; so to overcome this dilemma a special Act of Parliament was needed to appoint an interim Sheriff to act during Scott's incapacity. 'If it be necessary that an appointment of a Sheriff Substitute of Selkirk shd. take place soon', Lockhart told Willie a few weeks later, 'there is nothing to be said by me except that I don't entertain the remotest hope that Sir Walter Scott will be able to make it. The matter therefore is out of our hands': and he added in a footnote: 'In order to cut the matter short I have this day stated the case to the Lord Advocate.'[69] The Lord Advocate was Scott's old friend, Francis Jeffrey,* on whose proposal a Bill was passed to provide for the sick man's duties as Sheriff.

But the sheriffdom of Selkirk was soon vacant. On Friday September 21 at about half past one in the afternoon, Sir Walter Scott died. 'It was a beautiful day,' recorded his son-in-law in a well-known passage of his famous biography, 'so warm that every window was wide open—and so perfectly still that the sound of all others most delicious to his ear, the gentle ripple of the Tweed over its pebbles, was distinctly audible as we knelt by the bed, and his eldest son kissed and closed his eyes.'[70]

They buried him beside his wife in Dryburgh Abbey, and William Scott of Raeburn was one of the pall-bearers.

---

* Francis Jeffrey, Lord Jeffrey (1773–1850), distinguished advocate and judge, and one of the founders of *The Edinburgh Review* and was editor from 1803–39.

CHAPTER FOUR

William Scott of Raeburn and his children

T HE death of Cousin Walter must have been a sad blow
to Willie Scott. A friendship—partly fostered no doubt
by misfortune and sometimes nearly shattered by Raeburn's
idiosyncrasy, but genuine and heartfelt no whit the less—
had at last been broken; a man of vast influence and world-
wide renown was no longer at hand to help him in his per-
plexities, and they were many. But foremost among them
at the time of Sir Walter's death was how he was to provide
for his eldest son: this was a dreadfully difficult problem.
His good-natured brother, Robert, generous and kindly as he
was, was hardly a match for the cousin he had lost; and without him the poor man was thrown back upon his own resources. In the summer of 1832 Alexander's uncle Davidson* was
suggesting a trip to Paris. He invited the boy to stay with his
family in the French capital, and bade him ask his father's
leave. 'He says I may stay 6 weeks or 6 months as I like. It
would be a fine jaunt. He says I never will have such a good
opportunity of seeing the Continent . . . He is to leave in
10 or 12 days . . .'[1] Then again Mr Cleghorn, the family lawyer,
was against them trying to make Alexander into a ws and in
October he wrote to boy's father at considerable, indeed at
tedious, length to tell him so. He had three reasons: the profession was overcrowded, Alexander was now the eldest son and
would not want to carry on with the law after succeeding his
father, and thirdly, because he did not think his pupil's
abilities were of the kind to be usefully employed as a writer

---

* William Davidson of Muirhouse (in Cramond Parish, Midlothian)
married Jean Horsburgh, sister of Alexander's mother.

to the signet. At the same time he strongly urged Raeburn to apply to the Duke of Buccleuch for aid in obtaining a commission in the army for his son. 'It is quite obvious', Cleghorn wrote, 'that the late Sir Walter Scott, in the last edition of his works, was careful to shew that he was a *descendant* of the *family* of Raeburn . . . Alexander, if he lives, will be the representative of that family to which Sir Walter belonged . . . ' and in view of that he was certain that the Duke of Buccleuch would exert himself to do what he was asked. 'Sir Walter's name is now in every mouth, the Biographical notices of him have extracted from his works the parts connected with the family of Raeburn, and I am certain that from the friendship the Duke had for Sir Walter he will do what is necessary for putting the future representative of Raeburn in the army if his friends wish it . . .'[2] Robert assured Cleghorn that his brother proposed waiting upon the Duke shortly '. . . and the sooner you set about it the better', he told Willie, 'as on all occasions it is a good plan to strike the iron while it is hot, as the saying is . . .'[3] Yet despite this excellent advice, brother William did not bestir himself, preferring to wait for a reply to an application made to Lord Fitzroy Somerset,* at the same time insisting that he was making every possible effort on his son's behalf. 'While God spares me', he told Robert, 'I shall do all I can for [his] interest according to my circumstances', adding rather pathetically 'May God Almighty so prosper you, my dear Robert, is the fervent prayer of your ever affect. brother, in which Susan joins. W. Scott.'[4]

In due course Alexander had his interview with Lord Fitzroy, about which Robert was not optimistic. 'I hope something may be done for him but I must confess I am not very hopeful,'[5] he told his brother, and five weeks later, 'I much fear that all your applications to the great for aid in procuring a situation for Alexander will end in smoke, and I must confess that I hardly know what to advise you to do with regard to

* Lord Fitzroy James Henry Somerset (1788–1855) youngest son of the fifth Duke of Beaufort, created Lord Raglan.

him. . . .'[6] Whereupon, Willie and Susan Scott went off to
Harrogate for his health and did not return to Lessudden until
May when he pronounced himself to be better. Robert was
glad that he had returned to 'the old Castle' and that 'upon
the whole you considered your trip to Harrogate has been
beneficial to your health'.[7]

Alexander too does not seem to have been much encouraged
by his interview with the great man; and, weary of waiting in
London, he later in the month went off to visit Uncle Hugh
and Aunt Sarah at Draycott in company with Uncle Robert's
son-in-law, Church. They travelled by water from Edinburgh
to Glasgow—'a very tedious way of trawling [*sic*] as they go
no faster than a slow trot'—and then sailed by the Manchester
Steam Boat. It was a rough passage and there was 'lots of
sickness and throwing up, but wonderful to say I got over it
without being at all sick'; and so they reached Liverpool the
following evening. They travelled the next day to Derby by
stage coach, arrived about 8 o'clock in the evening. There
they stayed the night and reached Draycott for breakfast
next morning. 'Uncle Hugh and Mrs Scott desire their kind
regards.'[8] After a few days at Draycott, they returned to
London where Alexander lodged with 'a Mrs Bothwell, a
lady from Aberdeen and her daughter, who are very nice
people. They have seven or eight young men lodgers who
are all Scotchmen . . . The Lodgings are very cheap, only
£1:10: 0d. a week.' Then there follows a particularly modern
touch. 'There is no doubt but what London is a terrible place
for spending money, but I keep my purse as much closed as it
is in my power.' But he will not run out of cash, for Uncle
Robert has given him £10, Uncle Hugh £4 and he has £11 in
hand.[9] Meanwhile his father, in addition to having written
on his son's behalf to Lord Fitzroy Somerset, wrote also to
Lord Montagu who will, he hopes, see that the Duke of
Buccleuch and Lord John Scott are 'useful to you'. But
Alexander must send in his card to the duke and 'ask for his
principal man Metcalf[10] and say you are my son—for servants
often say nay without *master's orders*'.[11]

Now the object of all these manœuvres was for Alexander
to succeed a certain Mr Rutherford who was about to retire
from the army, and obtain his commission. This Rutherford
made a written statement of his intention which Alexander
took to Lord Munster,* adjutant-general at the Horse Guards.
Munster advised Alexander to leave the statement with him
and to attend Lord Fitzroy Somerset's *levée,* promising that
he would speak to him on the young man's behalf. Alexander
thought this good going and he seems to have ignored his
father's instructions to pay his respects to the Duke of
Buccleuch and Lord John Scott. 'I have neither seen the
Duke of Buccleuch nor Lord John', he told his father, 'and
can't be troubled running after them. I feel as indifferent as
they do now that I have got Lord Munster to speak on my
behalf, whose interest I think if used is better than either of
them.' He then turned to another subject. He had heard that
Ann Scott, the late Sir Walter's younger daughter, was very
ill with brain fever and some said that she was dead. He
concluded by promising to write again after seeing Lord
Fitzroy Somerset.[12]

So Alexander had a second interview with Lord Fitzroy;
and this was no more encouraging than the first. The great
man did not think that Rutherford could be allowed to retire
in his favour, and young Scott found it impossible to get out of
him a direct answer. 'He said he did not think it of any use
my staying in town any longer as Mr Rutherford's retiring
would not quicken the progress of my appointment.' Clearly
Alexander was getting thoroughly impatient and discouraged,
and he told his father that if he is not allowed to succeed
Rutherford he is 'quite determined not to wait. I don't know
what to do. Lord Fitzroy will not give a direct answer, he will
neither say that it is perfectly impossible nor that it can be
done. I am quite prepared to go to India or any other place

* George Augustus Frederick Fitzclarence, first Earl of Munster
(1794–1842), eldest child of the Duke of Clarence, afterwards
William IV, and Mrs Jordan.

else where I can get immediate employment as I think it is of no use living in uncertainty of a commission. . . .' And he ends on a sad note: 'you will have heard that the reported death of Miss Ann Scott is quite true. Mrs Lockhart is in a very bad state.'[13]

Meanwhile, his Uncle Robert, in bad health, had resolved to give up his house in Edinburgh and go to London. ' . . . nothing but trouble and difficulties in this miserable world . . .' he told Willie. 'Sister Barbara is of course distressed at the move and talks of looking for another house in Edinburgh, . . . but it is all *Bamboozle*,' he declares to his brother, 'it was never intended that we should have any resting place here below . . .' He is having his portrait packed up and sent to Lessudden, so that 'you can give it a birth in the Old Castle. . . .' and 'the young folks when we are dead and gone by and by will be able to say that is the picture of an old Uncle of theirs that was many years at Penang in the East Indies . . .'[14] Poor Uncle Robert was clearly failing.

Whilst Robert Scott was thus bemoaning the fate of mankind, his nephew was still in London trying in vain to get his commission. Following his unsatisfactory interview with Lord Fitzroy Somerset, he attended the *levée* of Lord Hill, the commander in chief in England,[15] whose tactics were rather different. '. . . he paid me so many compliments that I think he laid the butter on rather thick', Alexander told his father. 'He said that he did not know what to think about a Commission, that there were so many before me yet, that he was afraid I would have to wait some little time yet but that he would be very happy to serve me whenever it was in his power, that I was a very fine young man and a very gentlemanly young man &c. &c. . . .'[16] The same notes played in a different key!

Alexander was by now thoroughly wearied of wasting his time in London in a fruitless search for a commission which, it seems, could only be procured through somebody who had far more influence with the authorities than his poor weak father could ever hope for. Accordingly, he accepted his

uncle Davidson's suggestion to stay with him and his family
and try his luck in the French capital. The first thing he must
do is to learn the language and he proposed to stay with his
uncle's old tutor who had taken a house in Paris. His uncle
advised him to get into an Academy where he could become
qualified for the army and so have preference over those who
were not. Before leaving London, however, he called once
more upon Lord Munster in a last effort to get support for his
commission; but Munster had recently resigned his post of
adjutant general at the Horse Guards, and he frankly told his
applicant that he now had no influence.[17] 'I have not heard
a word about Alexander', wrote Uncle Robert, who had
settled temporarily at Hastings for his health,

> whether he went to London or not. If he did I conclude
> he would make but a brief stay there, prior to his leaving
> for Paris. Has his Uncle Davidson promised him his
> countenance while there or what does he propose to do?
> I should think he would find himself rather awkwardly
> situated among the *Petites* not being able to speak a word
> of their language. I hope he may be successful in his
> undertakings, but it is up hill work to make much
> progress in the world nowadays—however anything is
> better than being idle and I'm glad that Alexander views
> the matter in that light.[18]

Now the generous Robert had deposited £500 with the
British Linen Bank to purchase Alexander's commission if
he could get one; and Willie, worried about the expense of his
son attending a Military Academy, had cast loving eyes upon
these funds. But Robert was discouraging: it would, he
thought, be the height of imprudence to appropriate any part
for any other purpose whatsoever.[19] However, he sent his
nephew £50 to help him in Paris. 'He is one of the best of men',
that nephew told his father, 'there seems to be no end to his
kindness.' This unexpected gift was most welcome, for the
expenses of the Academy were more than he could afford.
The fee was only £75 a year, but the student had to supply
for himself such things as shirts, towels, knives, forks and

goblets, and in addition 'some money to pay upon entering'. In consequence of this Alexander followed his uncle Davidson's advice and went to live with his uncle's former tutor, a Mr Beauchere, who was on intimate terms with the Davidson family. 'I am the only person who lives with him . . . I pay £7 a month for board and education. I have liberty to attend all classes and lectures for the same money. I have a small room which is my bedroom and study. Aunt Jane* gave me shirts and towels. Mr Beauchere is exceedingly kind and gives me every thing that is in his power to make me comfortable, so I think I will live exceedingly happy with him and at the same time gain a great deal of information.' His uncle recommends him to study in the daytime and to go to parties at night, of which there are many, and introduces him to all his friends as his nephew and the cousin of Sir Walter Scott, 'and the French who are great admirers of Sir Walter Scott tell me that I have a beautiful name'.[20] But Robert Scott remains sceptical of all this expenditure. '. . . about your young folks, it is full time that things were off your hands . . .' he tells his brother, adding '. . . and as for Alexander . . . the Army is certainly a very expensive place for a young man . . .'[21] A month later he sends Willie £25 towards the expense of alterations and repairs to the old burial aisle at Lessudden, where nearly all their forbears are buried, adding *'keep this matter to yourself as I dislike much to have anything that I do talked about'*.[22]

For a time all seemed to go well for Alexander in Paris, but this good fortune soon came to a sudden end. Early in 1834 revolution broke out and the Davidson family were forced to beat a hasty retreat. For some time there had been unrest throughout the country and especially around Paris. And then suddenly this erupted into action: the workers of Lyons and elsewhere struck in protest against the severe new repressive laws, and after a bloody struggle lasting four days the military had to be called out to quell the Lyons mob. Then

---

* His mother's sister, wife of his 'Uncle Davidson'.

when the government ordered the arrest of a hundred and fifty Republicans the people of Paris revolted. On Sunday afternoon Paris was quiet as usual. But at about 5 o'clock when the Davidson family were at dinner, the old French servant rushed into the room to announce that a revolution had commenced, that there was firing nearby and that Louis Philippe was hemmed in on every side. All this proved somewhat exaggerated, but the beating of rebel drums to summon the troops made sleep impossible that night. By the next day the insurrection was crushed by the military forces led by Thiers himself and all was quiet once more. 'In Paris at present there are sixty thousand men under arms. I think that ought to keep order! but I don't think that sixty thousand Frenchmen could do so much as thirty thousand Englishmen, they are such a parcel of Tailor looking fellows.' So wrote Alexander to his father from his Uncle Robert's house in Hastings. 'I found Uncle Robert looking rather thin and complaining much of weakness and I think he is in low spirits and thinks himself worse than he is.'[23]

A few days later a cousin, George Scott, arrived and this 'raised Uncle Robert's spirit a little'. With the newcomer Alexander discussed the question of his going to India. George was strongly in favour, saying there was no better place in India than Penang for a young man who makes good use of his time. As good luck would have it there was a ship sailing in about seventeen days, 420 tons and commanded by an acquaintance of his Uncle Robert. But this would be a terrible rush, and Uncle Robert and George Scott suggest that, if Alexander decided to sail with her, there would be insufficient time to make it worth while his going north to say farewell to his parents; '. . . but, my dear Father, this is for your consideration, not theirs. I feel afraid that our meeting for such a short time would only make us worse when we are obliged to part, and I think that if you and Mama can make up your minds to allow me to go without seeing me, it would be better . . . It would be very painful for me to go away without seeing you all again but I think were we to meet for such a short time to part again would make me doubly worse. My dear Father,' he concluded pathetically, 'I hope that wherever I may go that I will always remain your affectionate obedient son, and it is just for you to say what you wish, and I am ready to do it . . .' Then he tells his father that the restless Uncle Robert has taken a house at Tunbridge Wells and moves there shortly, and that he will go with his uncle, but if his father agrees to his going to India, he and George will go to London together to make all necessary arrangements.[24]

A fortnight later Alexander and his uncle have moved to Tunbridge Wells, and the nephew has gone up to London to prepare for the journey. He asks his father to send him a box of things from Lessudden that he will need. Meanwhile, Uncle Robert has relented about the funds deposited with the British Linen Bank and has sent for a remittance of some money. 'He says that £200 of it will cover all my expenses and . . . that if I like to take the remaining £300 I ought to be able to get 8% for it upon good security . . . If I get every thing finished that I have got to do to-day, I intend to return to Tunbridge Wells tomorrow to take the Sacrament at your request . . .'[25]

The trunk duly arrived from Lessudden, and all was ready for Alexander to sail, not apparently by the ship already mentioned, but by the *Diana*, 500 tons, commanded by Captain Dudman: 'a very nice person indeed'. The passage money was £100. 'I am to have the cabin next the after cabin, which is I think 7 feet by 6 in size, which will be very comfortable . . . I am going down to the vessel which is in the eastern London dock to arrange about the putting up of my bed. I will have room for a fixed bed, and also for a small table and chair.' As soon as things are ready he will return to his uncle, who has changed his house in Tunbridge Wells. Meanwhile, his Uncle Hugh has written from Derbyshire inviting his nephew to stay before sailing and sending £50 to help his fitting out.[26] There was no time for the visit, but the gift was most welcome.

A few days later Alexander returned to Tunbridge Wells

to find his uncle depressed and alone. 'I have almost determined never to put pen to paper again . . . all seems so useless',
Robert told his brother.[27] '. . . Uncle Robert is much the same
as he has been for some time', reported his nephew who
thought him if anything somewhat better, 'because he takes
long walks and drives . . .' And he assured his father that
he was ready to sail.[28] The trouble with Uncle Robert was
that he was consulting a lot of books about his health and 'he
gets frightened and becomes convinced that he is going to
die, when in truth he is only slightly indisposed'. What he
needs, wrote his nephew, is some old friends to draw him out
of himself 'who can crack about there [*sic*] doings in India in
there [*sic*] younger days . . .'[29] He had taken a small cottage
near Tunbridge Wells called Broom Hill Cottage and he
proposed removing on July 1st for two or three months where
he 'can remain quiet and out of the way', he told his brother,
and then look for something in a warmer climate.[30] '. . . I have
almost determined to go out to Madeira, where I certainly
think I shall be much more comfortable than at either Brighton or Hastings', he told Willie a few weeks later, adding 'It
is a sad business to get kicked about in this measure . . . but
God's will be done'.[31] On November 18, some eleven weeks
later, he announced to Willie his safe arrival at Madeira.[32]

Meanwhile, Alexander had sailed for Penang in October,
as recorded sadly by his father in his Day Book;* and towards
the end of November he reported his safe arrival. There he
found his cousins Charles and Hugh Scott who gave him a
very kind reception; but as there was no room for another
with them he was accommodated with a room in a large
house occupied by Church: '. . . you will be sorry to hear that
Mr Church was Governer [*sic*] at Sincapore [*sic*] for a short
while, and again turned out, and he is living here doing
nothing . . .' He is delighted with Penang—'a beautiful place',
he tells his father, and thinks he will live there 'a very contented quiet life'.[33]

---

* He recorded it as October 1833, a mistake for 1834.

All was sadness now for the solitary laird of Raeburn. He
had lost his first-born six years ago in the *Acorn* disaster; his
second son was far away in a distant land, and perhaps they
would meet no more. He was crippled, his health was broken and
his thoughts now dwelt much on the past. In May he noted
that it was the anniversary of his sailing for India from St
Helens in the *Macarthy*, and in October of his first landing at
Penang forty years ago. News from Robert in Madeira was
depressing: 'I still continue in a sad state of debility', he
wrote home, 'but it is useless to say anything about that . . .'[34]
Willie replied in equally depressing terms: 'Alas, that I can
do but little to aid you in your distressed state further than
offering up my constant prayers to the Almighty to take you
into his Holy Keeping and not to lay more upon you than
you are enabled to bear . . .'[35] Robert remained in Madeira for
another twelve months, writing in July of the following year
to his eldest niece Violet his sorrow that her father's health
had not improved, and adding 'I am thank God, free from
pain, but can do nothing . . .'[36] Shortly after the date of this
letter Robert Scott returned to London and early in September
poor Willie had to record that he had lost his 'very dear and
beloved brother'. 'You may judge the state of my feelings',
wrote Barbara, 'when I found that our Dear Brother Robert
had paid the debt of nature on Sunday the 4th. This day his
mortal remains are to be laid in their narrow house in a
Burial Ground belonging to Mr Burnie, where they can be
removed again at any time if his relations have a wish to do
so. God's will be done, heavy as his afflicting hand has fallen
upon us . . .'[37]

All was sadness now at Lessudden. Yet Willie Scott loved
his home; and now that at last he had inherited a quite
considerable fortune from his parsimonious father, he determined to devote himself to improving his estate and to
enlarging the modest building so as the more suitably to
accommodate his family. On October 20 he laid the foundation
stone of the new west wing of Lessudden House, and he duly
recorded this momentous event in his Day Book.

He must have been heartened and encouraged by a letter from Alexander saying that he had gone into business at Penang and thanking his father for all he was doing to improve the Estate for him. '. . . but I hope that we may still live to meet again. I am doing very well at Penang and would like in two or three years more to make a business voyage home if I can manage to make the business pay the way . . .' He is glad that his younger brothers, Robert and William, are getting on well and he hopes that 'we may succeed in getting them on well with the world that they may be able in due time to do for themselves.' He has had a letter from Robert and is glad that he writes so well, '. . . but I hope you will not think of making him a Farmer in Scotland which appears to me to be not so good as many things he might do . . .' As for William, who hopes to be a doctor: 'If he can be a Doctor and get into the Company's service that would be a fine thing for him . . .'[38]

It was at about this time and amidst the accumulating sorrows of his later life that the solitary laird at Lessudden began to become intimate with a friend and adviser of long standing—not perhaps so influential as his great cousin, Sir Walter, but not to be disparaged. She was the wife of his kinsman, Hugh Scott of Harden.

CHAPTER FIVE

Harriet Polwarth and the Scotts of Raeburn

THE fortunes of the Harden Scotts had greatly fluctuated over the years. In 1659 the ambitious Sir Gideon Scott of Highchester, a grandson of the old freebooter Wat of Harden,* pulled off a remarkable coup. He arranged a marriage between his eldest son Walter and the immensely wealthy Lady Mary Scott, in her own right Countess of Buccleuch. The ceremony took place in February, 1659 when the bridegroom was fourteen and the bride eleven; and Sir Gideon was one of the curators of the two minors. Not unnaturally these unseemly events created a great stir, and the provincial Synod of Fife discussed an accusation brought against the presbytery of having granted a warrant for the marriage without proclamation. The presbytery was, however, absolved from all blame on the grounds that the order was grounded upon an act of the General Assembly allowing such marriages in cases of necessity, and that the necessity was present in this case because her friends were apprehensive that the child bride was in danger of being carried off and raped. So much for Sir Gideon's reputation. But though the marriage was valid, the civil authorities saw fit to intervene and to separate the young couple until little Lady Buccleuch had completed her twelfth year, when she ratified what had been done. Meanwhile, the shameless Sir Gideon was anxious that his son should assume his wife's proud title of Buccleuch; but that was more than the authorities could stomach, and the bridegroom had to be content with the high-sounding but empty dignities of Earl of Tarras and Lord Almoor and Campeastill, all for

---

* A younger brother of Walter the first laird of Raeburn.

life only. Then, when at the very summit of success, a totally unexpected event brought all Sir Gideon Scott's schemes to naught. In March, 1661 the child bride died leaving no issue.* Long and costly legal proceedings ensued, at the end of which the young widower found his marriage contract varied, and himself disappointed of the provision set apart for him out of his wife's vast property. At intervals during the reign of Charles II, Lord Tarras continued his endeavours to persuade the Sovereign to grant him a provision out of the Buccleuch Estates, but the king was adamant and all efforts to move him were vain. Towards the end of the reign Tarras became involved in the plots to exclude the Duke of York from the throne, was found guilty of treason and sentenced to death. He was more fortunate than many: not only was his life spared, but he subsequently recovered his honours and his lands. This was of special consequence to him because on the last day of 1677, by which time he was thirty-three, he had made a second marriage. His bride was Helen, daughter of Thomas Hepburne of Humbie, and by her he had no less than five sons and six daughters. A century and a half later Helen's great-great-grandson assumed her surname in addition to his own in consequence of the estates of the Hepburnes of Humbie having descended to him through the Countess of Tarras. Lord Tarras died in April 1693, when his life peerage expired with him.

Thus the hopes and ambitions of the unscrupulous Sir Gideon Scott of Highchester were disappointed. But some sixty years later the fortunes of the Scotts of Harden were revived once more when Tarras's grandson, Walter Scott of Harden, married Lady Diana Hume Campbell, third daughter of the third and last Earl of Marchmont. Lady Diana Scott

---

* She was succeeded by her sister Lady Anne Scott as Countess of Buccleuch, and on her marriage to the ill-fated Duke of Monmouth in 1663 husband and wife were created jointly Duke and Duchess of Buccleuch. They were also Duke and Duchess of Monmouth, the dukedom bestowed on the husband a few weeks earlier.

of Harden subsequently became *de jure* Baroness Polwarth.*

It was the wife of the only son of this marriage,** Hugh
Scott of Harden, who was to prove the second prop and stay
in the life of Willie Scott of Raeburn. It was well for both
Harden and Raeburn that the former had prevailed upon the
right woman to become his wife, for he too, it seems, was of
an irresolute nature. 'I have known Harden long and most
intimately—', Walter Scott told the Duke of Buccleuch early
in 1817, 'a more respectable man either in feeling, or talent, or
knowledge of human life, is rarely to be met with. But he is
what the ladies call a *dawdler,* habitually irresolute or rather
indecisive and requiring generally some instant stimulus in
order to make him resolve to do, not only what he knows to be
right, but what he really wishes to do, and means to do one
time or other. He is exactly Prior's Earl of Oxford:

> *Let that be done which Mat doth say—*
> *"Yea"—quoth the Earl—"but not today".*

However he wishes you well—thinks highly of your Grace
and rather regrets he is not better acquainted with you.'[1]
With so procrastinating a nature, it was highly desirable that
Scott of Harden should marry a strong-minded young lady
who would have in her make-up what was needful to counter
his weakness. And by rare good fortune that is precisely
what he had done. 'We have a great marriage towards here',
Walter Scott had written to Willie Clerk back in 1795, 'Scott
of Harden, and a daughter of Count Bruhl, the famous chess-
player, a lady of sixteen quarters, half-sister to the Wyndhams.
I wish they may come down soon, as we shall have fine
racketing, of which I will, probably, get my share.'[2] Count
Bruhl of Martikirchen had for long been Saxon ambassador
at the Court of St James's and his daughter Harriet was by

---

* It was as representing through his mother the line of Marchmont
that Scott of Harden's right to the peerage of Polwarth was
allowed by the House of Lords in 1835.
** There had been a previous child, Walter, but he died an infant.

his second wife, the Dowager Countess of Egremont. She was, it seems, a girl of many parts. Young Walter Scott was introduced to her at Mertoun and a fast friendship ensued. She supplied him with many German books and as Mrs Scott of Harden read and criticised a month before its appearance Scott's *Ballad of the Wild Huntsman*, which was said to be a translation or rather an imitation of *Der Wilde Jäger* of the German poet Burger to whose work she had introduced Walter Scott.* She was, Scott used to say, the first woman of real fashion who took him up. 'When I first saw Sir Walter,' she told his biographer in after years, 'he was about four or five-and-twenty, but looked much younger. He seemed bashful and awkward; but there were from the first such gleams of superior sense and spirit in his conversation, that I was hardly surprised when, after our acquaintance had ripened a little, I felt myself to be talking with a man of genius.' This of course was many years later, so Harriet was writing with hind-sight to aid her. 'He was most modest about himself, and showed his little pieces apparently without any consciousness that they could possess any claim or particular attention. Nothing so easy and good-humoured as the way in which he received any hints I might offer, when he seemed to be tampering with the King's English. I remember particularly how he laughed at himself, when I made him take notice that "the little two dogs", in some of his lines, did not please an English ear accustomed to "the two little dogs".'[3]

But Harden's wife was not the only one at Mertoun to take notice of young Walter Scott; Harden's aged mother, Lady Diana Scott, did so no less. This highly cultured woman must have entranced the romantic young man with her recollections of the great literary figures who had survived the days of

---

* 'A lady of noble German descent, whose friendship I have enjoyed for many years, found means to procure me a copy of Burger's works from Hamburgh. . . .' *Introductory Note to Ballads from the German*, Scott's *Poetical Works* (ed. Logie Robertson, 1894), 651.

Queen Anne long enough to talk to her,* enraptured the budding poet with her somewhat unreliable reminiscences of one of the most eminent of their number, Alexander Pope.** She lived into her nineties; and many years later Sir Walter Scott records dining with his cousin at Maxpoffle with Sir Sidney Beckwith and his kinsman Hugh Scott of Harden, and that the mothers of his host and the other two guests were all still living:

		died
Mrs Beckwith	95	97
Lady Diana Scott	91	92
Mrs Scott of Raeburn	89	92

A truly remarkable record.

It was presumably through Sir Walter that Willie Scott became acquainted with this interesting person, but it was not until after his cousin's death that their friendship developed into anything approaching intimacy. Indeed, the earliest surviving letter from her to Raeburn is dated 1838, and most of these early ones were of family news. In 1840 she wrote to Raeburn that her daughter-in-law, 'poor Mrs Scott is of an immense size and I sh'd suppose must be confined ere long, and I am sorry she is rather nervous and fearful about herself owing to her spirits having been so much shaken.'[4] A year later she wrote to announce that her son William's wife had given birth to 'a fine little *black headed* Boy on the 11th of this month. His arrival was followed by that of a little girl but she, poor little soul, only lived a few hours, long enough for her Father to baptise her'; this was perhaps all for the best as the William Scotts had three girls already.†

---

* Queen Anne died in 1713, Lady Diana was born in 1735.
** She was only nine when Pope died, so she could not really have had any clear recollection of him.
† Lady Polwarth, February 16 [1841] to Mrs Scott of Raeburn. Raeburn Papers, SRO Box 8. Her son, the Rev. William Hugh Scott, rector of Maiden Newton, Dorset, had married Elinor Sophia, daughter of the Rev. Charles Baillie-Hamilton, uncle of the Earl of Haddington. The baby, christened William George, became a naval Commander and died in 1881.

But grandchildren for Lady Polwarth were two a penny at this time. In 1845 she wrote to announce the birth of a daughter for the wife of her eldest son Henry* and again shortly afterwards for her daughter Elizabeth. 'We are all well and I am in daily expectation of a new grandchild's arrival at C. Wyndhams',** she told Willie, 'Henry's wife is rather stronger and better at Granton, and he hopes to bring her home the beginning of next week.' Meanwhile, life at Harden was not too comfortable. 'Our household has been long in a state of chaos with a new chimney built at the North end in Henry's dressing room and a new ceiling made in the room at the South East end of the passage, so that neither room is in a habitable state and all their neighbouring spaces are filled with furniture.'[5]

Willie Scott was, it seems, a great reader and an enthusiastic collector of autographs.† Curiously enough, though his cousin must have been in the way of obtaining examples of the writing and signatures of countless notable people, Sir Walter Scott does not seem to have encouraged these enthusiasms; so perhaps we may conclude that Willie took up these hobbies in later life, when he was infirm and for some years confined to the house. Be that as it may, Lady Polwarth was frequently sending him books, advising him what to read and procuring him autographs. 'I send for your collection of autographs one of an excellent and particularly dear old lady who is 83 this August, and who is my oldest friend and was the much valued friend of Sir Walter Scott, Lady Louisa Stuart, the youngest

---

* Lady Polwarth, Thursday evening, February 20 [1845] to William Scott of Raeburn, Lessudden Place, Raeburn Papers, SRO Box 9. She was Georgina, daughter of George Baillie of Jerviswood and Mellerstain, and sister of the Earl of Haddington.
** Her daughter Elizabeth Anne was the wife of Colonel Charles Wyndham, MP, of Rogate, Sussex.
† William Scott's autograph book, starting with that of the first Raeburn in 1680, his signature witnessed by Thomas Lawrie, Indweller [in Lessudden] and William Bennet [Raeburn's Servitor]. Witnesses, can still be seen. NLS MS 3843.

daughter of the Earl of Bute, Minister of George III, and the gd. daughter (by the Mother's side) of Lady Mary Wortley Montagu'.[6] On another occasion she sends 'a note from the Duke of Marlborough (Father of the last absurd man) a very good and learned man but not famous in any way.'[7] Towards the end of the same year she wrote again: 'I send you Lord Home's letter to add to your collection and I send also a Foreign signature of an Italian who was many years Prime Minister to the old King of Saxony—the last and the first King—in case you like to have any Foreign ones. The letter is written by a Secretary to my Father, and Count Marcolini's signature you will see at the end.'[8] And sending Willie that year some 'old documents which I have found in my Father's Papers, which you may read and return some day', she added —no doubt to his astonishment—that 'the oldest memorable thing that I remember are [*sic*] Lord Geo. Gordon's riots in 1782 which immediately followed those letters which I send you.'[9] Lord George Gordon's No Popery riots were in the summer of 1780, sixty-one years before this letter was written: Lady Polwarth's inaccuracy in this detail prompts one to wonder how much she really could recall of those stirring events of long ago.

The first edition of Lockhart's famous biography of his father-in-law appeared in 1837–8, and in it were revealed Sir Walter's harsh but not unmerited comments upon his uncle, the late Walter Scott of Raeburn. When his father was alive, Willie had never been on good terms with him; but now that he was dead—blood being thicker than water—the son was somewhat distressed at his cousin's disparaging remarks appearing in print. He sent an advance copy of the biography to Harriet. Unfortunately the volume was taken to Lord Polwarth who promptly began to read it, using Willie's note as a bookmarker without realising that it was a letter. Consequently there was some delay before his wife received it which 'drop'd out of the Book while Lord P. was reading it and I believe it had served him as a place keeper for several days, and he had never discovered that it was not some old letter, so it is lucky that I got it at all.' Lady Polwarth was anxious to soothe her friend and to restrain him from further action. '. . . pray forgive me for saying that I think it were better to say or write nothing more about it. The word *Brute is used* certainly, but it is merely used by Sir Walter *calling forth* the *angry* feelings of *his own boyish* days about the *starling* and he was also at that time harassed with ill health and worried with vexations so that his temper was sour'd— but I do not think that he bore any *ill will* at *that time* to your *Father* altho' he *recollected* the anger of his boyish days.'[10] That, we may think, was making the best of it; but as in the second edition of his famous biography Lockhart, who seldom took advice from anyone, omitted the word 'brute', it looks as if he must have done so after some very strong objections from Willie.

At about this time Willie received a letter from his son Alexander in Penang saying that certain members of the family were going to settle at King George's Sound on the west coast of Australia. He himself, however, was well content with Penang, where he was prospering. If only he could tell his father to send Robert or William out to him, but unfortunately there was no room in the office. However, as Robert wants to be a farmer, New South Wales is the place for him: '. . . it's an absolute fact', he tells his father, 'that every body who are good for any thing are making fortunes . . .'[11] But apparently, however keen he was to farm, Robert had no wish to go to Australia, for a few months later we find Alexander writing home this time suggesting that brother Robert should come out to Penang to join him. Early in the following year Robert sailed to join his brother, and there was more sadness for the old folks at Lessudden. 'Robert left Lessudden to go to Penang per *Chippawa*', recorded his father on February 19. She was due to sail on March 15, but six days later she was dismasted—'mixan mast cut away and main and foremast fell over', and she returned to Greenwich for repairs. These could not have been serious for the *Chippawa* sailed on the 25th and no further mishaps are recorded. But a sorrowing old father and mother must have been anxious for their boy's safety.

At home there was now but one son left; Willie and Susan's youngest son, William Hugh, and for him his father took a momentous decision: for once he would do something for himself. We have seen how many years ago he had tried to persuade his influential cousin to approach the Duke of Wellington on his behalf and had met with a blank refusal. He now resolved upon the bold step of writing himself to the duke to ask on behalf of his youngest son, aged seventeen, an ensign's commission in a foot regiment.[12] He reminded his Grace that he had been with his regiment the 33rd at Penang in the year 1797 when Willie, a resident merchant, had met him at friends' houses. Later, when he was back in Scotland, he had met the duke in his cousin James Scott's house and elsewhere. He recorded that he returned home in 1805, married and had twelve children to provide for. Lord Hill, the Commander-in-Chief in England, had promised to place the name of his son William Hugh 'stout and healthy' on the list, and Lord Fitzroy Somerset, Secretary at the Horse Guards, had advised him to address his Grace on the subject.* So he now wrote to solicit the ensignship for his son. 'If W.S.'s full cousin Sir Walter Scott had been living', he told the duke, 'this favour would have been probably solicited by him.'** 'I am now a great invalid and have been confined to the house for five years' he continued, 'Should your Grace wish to enquire about me, I think I can take the liberty of saying the Duke of Buccleuch knows me, and so did his father better, and his grandfather . . . and I think the Marquis of Lothian, five miles from this, knows our standing in the country.' Alas! the appeal was fruitless. The duke replied that since he relinquished the office of Commander-in-Chief

---

* Lord Fitzroy Somerset was of course an intimate of Wellington's and was married to his niece.
** This was frankly dishonest, for he could hardly have forgotten that on a former occasion his cousin had refused to solicit the duke.

he had never interfered in any matter connected with the
army except in cases where his advice and assistance had
been sought.[13]

This disappointment was swiftly followed by another. We
have seen how Alexander had assured his father that he was
prospering in Penang and had persuaded him to let Robert
come out and join him. Thus Robert duly arrived in the early
summer of 1838 and, no doubt realising that Alexander's
position was less secure than he had represented it to be, had
gone on to Singapore to try his fortune there. The truth was
that Alexander was changing his employment and about to
go into partnership with a fellow Scott. This proved a great
failure and after only some four months of partnership Alexander left the firm because his partner had admitted a stranger
into the firm without his consent. Whereupon, Alexander sued
his partner and was awarded compensation of some £400
sterling. 'What a mortification it must be to them [i.e. the
firm] to find that I have obliged them to give me almost
everything that I asked . . .' he told his father: furthermore,
Messrs. Scott had to pay the expenses of the application
estimated at about £200. '. . . I think I will leave for Singapore
to see Robert. I have some idea of either returning here or
staying there as Merchant on my own account . . .'[14] Also in
Singapore, in addition to Robert, was Willie's cousin, another
William Scott, and when this William gave Robert a helping
hand, Robert's father wrote to thank his cousin. This delighted
William in Singapore who had not met the laird of Raeburn
for many years, and he wrote to deplore Willie's ill-health.
'The Society of your Daughters must have been a great
support to you', he told him. 'You will laugh at what I am
going to say but I fear I shall give offence to my Cousins when
I express my apprehension of their retreating on your family
a pair of old maids by not attending to the advice of two pairs
of Misses Scotts of Harden and Thirlestane who recommended
to my sisters not to be shy but to meet the men half long.' But
the advice of the Misses Scotts does not seem to have been
particularly good, for he adds, 'Two of my sisters unhappily

followed their advice and made runaway marriages. One of the Miss Scotts of Harden was firmly attached to the great unknown's father.'[15] One wonders how these somewhat personal remarks were received by the elderly couple at Lessudden.

Early in 1840 Willie and Susan had to suffer the departure for Australia of their youngest son, William Hugh. 'January 22nd, 1840', recorded the sorrowing father, 'our dear William left Lessudden for Edinburgh and Greenock on his way to Australia . . . sailed February 17.' So all the boys had left home. The first born son perished at sea; the second and third sons were at Penang; and the youngest was now sailing for Australia. Only daughters were at home to keep their parents company.

The Borders were a gay place for young ladies in early Victorian times, and in the autumn of 1840 there were many balls for them to attend. 'Anne went from Mellerstain to Floors and back in her Britska', Harriet Polwarth told Willie, 'which not having been shut during the rain of Friday night, got wet through and she got a rheumatism in her head and neck in going back to Fleurs with which she still suffers a good deal.' Poor Anne Scott, but it was all in a good cause— a ball in Kelso town and another at the Castle.

My Daughters Anne and Francis' wife were very sorry to hear two of your Daughters were at the Kelso Ball unknown to them, as the room was so extremely full that they never saw them, as they would have been most happy to have been of any use to them if in their power. And *I am rather angry with you* for *not letting us know* your Daughters *were going* to one of the Kelso Balls and that they *were invited* to Floors, *where it is a great pity they did not go and we think* you might have entrusted them to be chaperoned either by Anne or Julia* (Francis'

---

* Julia Frances Laura, daughter of the Rev. Charles Boultbee by his wife Laura, sister and sole heir of George, fourth and last Earl of Egremont.

wife) altho' she is so short sighted (almost blind) that she had no chance of seeing them if they did not speak to her, Francis and Julia had a lodging at Kelso and could and would have been most happy to have been of use.[16]

But the Scott of Raeburn girls had gone to both balls—not much to their satisfaction, as their father wrote to his friend. 'Before Susan and Barbara went to Kelso I wrote to Miss MacDougall as a concession requesting that she wd. have the goodness to introduce our daughters to their graces of Roxh. and had a kind reply saying that if they wd. go to the stand she wd. do so.' But when the time came Miss Mac-Dougall had other things to claim her attention and she forgot all about the two Scott girls. Then Mrs Kerr of Gateshaw promised to introduce Susan and Barbara. But she too failed them. 'Mrs K. then sd. to B. "I hope you have found your party, Miss Scott," in rather a high manner and left them. Thus they sat unknown and of course not noticed and became so disheartened that they left before supper and came home next day, sending an excuse to the Duchess.' Poor girls: one can sympathise with them. 'They must stay at home in future,' wrote their father adding sadly 'Our old friends have vanished or this wd. not have happened.'[17]

As usual poor Willie was counting on others to help him. But he was old and infirm now, and his thoughts dwelt more and more on trivia and events of long ago. In January 1839 'the scarlet thorn planted by my late brother John blown up in a heavy gale of wind from the west'. He immediately raised and tied it up again, and on May 1 he recorded that it began to show leaf. Again in January of the following year it was blown down for the second time: but he righted it, and in mid-April he noted that it was beginning to show leaf a fortnight earlier than the previous year.

Meanwhile, Harriet Polwarth tried to rally the old man from his depression and to stimulate his interest in the domestic events in her family. Elizabeth Wyndham's eldest boy has had scarlet fever very mildly, the nurse more seriously, but they are both on the mend. The great secret for good

health, she says, is keeping one's house warm. Lord Polwarth
is aging and more or less confined to the ground floor now, so
'we keep all the rooms on the ground floor equally warm, for
him to move about when he is able'. No doubt the Scotts
keep Lessudden warm too 'for the comfort of others as well
as yourself, and it is the *best economy too* to *keep away illness.*'
But there is one difficulty: 'I cannot keep the stairs here
tolerably warm'.[18] Later that year the Scotts had invited their
friend to lunch on the day of the St Boswells' annual fair,
but alas! she could not manage it, for 'where either *very* old
or *very* young are concerned one is not master of one's own
time.' Her husband demands much of her attention; but as
he now allows his valet to assist him in dressing she is free
earlier than of yore, 'which made me take time by the *Forelock*
at *11 o'clock* on Monday morning to drive through the Fair
and we thought we had better dispatch the Children's going
there with me before their nap (at least Walter's) and their
dinner'. To this letter Raeburn appended a note: 'The Lady
Polwarth—an acquaintance of 41 years standing and one of
the truest and best of friends—*always the same.*'[19] Later that
year she has to repeat that another young member of the
family is down with scarlet fever, this time Anne's[20] daughter
Rachel: 'our little invalid is most surprisingly well but the
wise people say much care is required *after* the S. Fever and
also that the infection continues altho' the person appears to
be quite well, as long as there is still *any old skin* to *peal,* and
little Rachel's skin her mother tells me, is in the *act of pealing*
now, so the quarantine continues and the other children
keep well.'[21]

The Polwarths were much in London now, and Harriet
was wont to send her old friend at Lessudden the latest news
of events of interest in the capital. Thus after the bedchamber
question on the resignation of Lord Melbourne in 1839, when
Sir Robert Peel claimed the right to recommend to the young
queen certain changes in her household, superseding some of
her ladies who were thought to be too closely connected with
the outgoing ministers, and Queen Victoria objected, the

matter was more or less amicably settled in 1841 through the intervention of Baron Stockmar and Prince Albert. She reported to Raeburn that 'The Queen is allowed to keep all her ladies here except the Dss. of Sutherland and Lady Normanby,'[22] and again some two years later: 'You would admire Sir Robert Peel's last speech and Mr Gladstone's also —that beast Mr Cobden is *quite a nuisance*. He is a Midhurst man* of whom Ch. Wyndham has a great horror.'[23] At the end of 1841 Harriet Polwarth had particularly sad news to record: Lord Polwarth died on December 29 in his eighty-fourth year.

Following his retirement from Messrs Scott's Alexander went to Singapore to see Robert and to consider the possibility of becoming a merchant on his own account either there or at Penang. Nothing seems to have come of these plans and by the summer of 1842 he was home again and looking for work. His father, of course, instead of doing something himself, applied to the widowed Lady Polwarth to try to procure for him a government post. Lady Polwarth was naturally anxious to help her old friend, but 'I *dare not hope* on the subject, for there are so many more applicants than places and I fear your son being the eldest and the heir to a patrimony in Scotland, altho' not a large one, will stand against him, for there are so many young men who have actually *nothing nor are* in expectation, and all governments like to employ them as they are more dependent on them, provided they are *qualified to do their work*.' However she had consulted her son Francis, who had been a member of parliament before succeeding to his father's peerage, to see what he could do: but there were innumerable applicants 'from all sorts of people for all

---

* Richard Cobden (1804–1865) was born near Midhurst in Sussex. 'He came of an ancient stock of yeomen of the soil, for several centuries rooted in that district.' (DNB)

sorts of things, and all the poor little MPs who have like him very *little* influence, are I dare say equally applied to'. So much for the back bench MP in the middle of the last century!

Lady Polwarth was staying with the Wyndhams in Sussex at the time and she thus recorded the discomforts of travel in the nineteenth century.

> We had a tiresome journey hither waiting an hour before the *Train* started. The day was stormy like a hurricane and at about 16 miles South of London the engine became useless, would not *burn, boil or move*. So we had to wait another hour till another engine was brought and *all the while* in a fright lest another train should come up and *bounce* against us, but at last it [the engine] came and we got on to where we had to take to our own carriages and we had not proceeded far before the front Dickey* of Col. Wyndham's carriage *broke,* but luckily no accident happened to any one, and they were stowed in our 2 carriages as *best we could* . . .[24]

But Alexander Scott must be helped if possible, and, as certain appointments were due to be made shortly in China, the new Lord Polwarth wrote to Lord Aberdeen, the Foreign Secretary in Sir Robert Peel's government, on his behalf. Aberdeen replied from the Foreign Office in typical evasive terms—nothing yet decided; it would give him pleasure to be of service; but he was unable at present to make any engagements—in short, a letter 'which I could have wished had been more decidedly favourable', wrote Polwarth to Raeburn, but one may hope that being known to Sir Henry Pottinger** Alexander has as fair a chance as others of getting some of the good things of China.'[25]

In May this year there was a ball at Lessudden for Raeburn's daughters, and we may hope that it was some consolation to Susan and Barbara for the fiasco at Floors. At any rate

---

* Dickey or dickey-box. The seat in a carriage on which the driver sits, or at the back for servants, or of a mail coach for the guard.
** Sir Henry Pottinger (1789–1856), soldier and diplomatist, had just been made the first governor of Hong Kong.

Harriet Polwarth wrote from the Wyndhams' house in London to congratulate the laird on its success. She had heard from her son Henry, she told him, how well it had gone off and that 'every lady danced with much spirit'. Then she turned to her own movements, for 'I have been a great traveller in this part of England'. She had spent three weeks with son William at his rectory and staying with Lord Egremont who has 'a large unfinished House which I wish *may* be comfortable if *ever* he accomplishes finishing it'. William's rectory was perfect, but the weather vile and the winds in Dorset had been very cold. With Elizabeth and her husband she was very comfortable: 'this is quite a new part of the Town so clean and airy that it is quite *unlike* London, and so near the south side of Hyde Park that it is almost like being in the Country', she wrote from Chester Street, off Grosvenor Place. London had been very empty but was filling up since the funeral of the Duke of Sussex,* who had died on April 21st. 'I suppose', commented Lady Polwarth, 'people thought there wd. be no gay doings till after that, and saved themselves the expence of deep mourning.' The Duke as a young man had created a great pother by marrying contrary to the provisions of the Royal Marriage Act of 1772 Lady Augusta Murray, a daughter of the fourth Earl of Dunmore; and, after her death, as an old man he repeated the offence by contracting a second marriage with Lady Cecilia Buggin, a daughter of the Earl of Arran and widow of Sir George Buggin. In 1840 this lady was created Duchess of Inverness. As if the Duke had not given his relations sufficient trouble in his life-time, when he died three years later he directed in his will that his remains should not be interred with the royal family at Windsor but in the public cemetery at Kensal Green. 'It is thought that his wish . . . was to have the Dss. of Inverness buried beside him,' commented Harriet Polwarth, 'which certainly is very *tender and pretty,* and the Queen could not with propriety have

* Augustus Frederick, Duke of Sussex (1773–1843), sixth son and ninth child of King George III and Queen Charlotte.

promised to bring her in the Royal Vault.' Then she added
unkindly, 'Poor man, he does not make much *blank* in the
world excepting that of his ponderous *size*!'[26]

A fortnight later, the young Lord Polwarth wrote to Raeburn about his son Alexander's prospects. He had spoken to
Alec. Pringle and the Duke of Buccleuch had given vague
assurances; but he had not had an opportunity of speaking to
Lord Aberdeen, the man who really counted. But he learnt
'respecting the appointments of consuls in China they were
extremely exacting and very anxious to find those who understood and spoke the language.'[27] It is extremely unlikely that
young Scott possessed this necessary qualification: nevertheless, in the autumn Raeburn was able to announce the joyful
news of Alexander's appointment. Harriet Polwarth, naturally
delighted, wrote from Brighton to congratulate both father
and son. 'I beg my kindest congratulations to Mrs Scott and
all your daughters on Alexander's good prospects', she wrote,
'and shall be very happy when I hear you have any satisfactory
accounts from yr. younger sons.'[28] But Raeburn's joy at his
son's appointment as consul was soon turned to sorrow. In
the autumn he sailed to start his new career in China; but
before the year was out he was dead. He was only thirty.

It does not seem as if the family at Lessudden heard much
from their old friend for a while—no further letter from her
has been found for the next eighteen months but in January
1845 she wrote to Willie from Rogate on a somewhat personal
subject.

> I rather wonder that any friend of your Daughters shd.
> have wished to make them acquainted with Lady Boling-
> broke who is not *good for much* (to say no worse) and
> indeed the whole family of Bolingbroke from the clever
> worthless Ld. B. in Queen Anne's time* are rather to be
> *shun'd* than *sought*. The present Lady B.** is hardly

---

* Henry St John, first Viscount Bolingbroke (1678–1751).
** Isabella Charlotte Antoinette Sophia Baroness Hompesch,
widow of the fourth Viscount. Their first child was born in 1804
two and a half months after their marriage.

visited except by *those* who prefer *rank* to *reputation,* and *my old acquaintance* Genl. St John* whom you may have *heard* of in *India* who was saved by Lord Lake's** *good nature* from being *turned out* of the *army* for preferring the *safety* of a *Ditch* to *exposing himself,* and who died at Brighton lately was no great *ornament* to the Family.'[29]

After this outburst, Harriet Polwarth seems to have remained silent for a while; but towards the end of this same year her son reported to Raeburn as one who 'rejoices in any mark of favour from the Crown being shown to the House of Harden', that he had been appointed Lord Lieutenant of Selkirkshire.[30] And just over a year later his mother was sending Willie Scott her New Year Greetings to which letter he has penned the words '1st January 1847, Dowager Lady Polwarth, one of the great and good. W.S.'[31] This was followed six days later by the joyful news from her son that his wife had given birth to their second son, that the mother had had an excellent night, and that 'the young gent is doing as well as I could wish a young Scott to do at so early a stage of his existence'.[32]

In the spring of 1847 more bad news came from the East. William Hugh in Singapore had managed to get himself appointed to the post of Master Attendant and Postmaster. This he held for some years when he was suddenly relieved of his duties by a certain Captain R. S. Ross, at the same time being ordered to carry on as Ross's assistant. To sugar this bitter pill he was promised a pension. The letter conveying this disagreeable intelligence was signed 'T. Church, Resident Councillor';[33]—possibly the same person of that name who has already been met with in these pages. At first William Scott showed himself willing to swallow his pride and accept these humiliating instructions. But when some two months later

---

* Presumably General the Hon. Frederick St John (1765–1819), second son of the third Viscount.
** Gerard, first Viscount Lake of Delhi and Leswarree (1744–1808), General, saw much service in India, a very charming and popular officer.

Church wrote again, this time to advise him that the decision on the pension had been reversed,[34] the unfortunate victim appealed to the Deputy Governor of Bengal. The only result of that move seems to have been that the ex-Master Attendant and Postmaster was informed that he was not up to his duties, that his pay had been reduced, and that he must refund the sums that had been erroneously paid to him. Though obviously monstrously unfair, it does not seem as if Scott obtained any relief, though how or when the government received its money—if it ever did—history does not relate.

At the same time that the poor old laird at Lessudden was worrying about his son's future, he received news that his cousin Sir Walter Scott's elder son—the second Sir Walter, who had become a Lieutenant Colonel in the 15th Hussars— had been invalided out of the army and had died on board ship on his way home. He and Jane had had no children, so the baronetcy became extinct.* His sister Anne, as we have already seen, had died in June, 1833, less than a year after her father. His sister Sophia Lockhart had died in 1837, and his younger brother Charles had died a bachelor at Tehran in October 1841. So poor Willie Scott of Raeburn had outlived not only his dear cousin, but all four of that cousin's children.

When Harriet Polwarth was staying with the Wyndhams in London in 1849 she complained that 'I am very far from well, with this horrid influenza'. Then she turned to public affairs. She greatly regretted Lord John Russell's advice to the queen to appoint Dr Hampden** to the bishopric of

---

* It was revived in 1932 by King George V to commemorate the centenary of Sir Walter Scott's death, when Sir Walter's great-great-grandson became Major-General Sir Walter Maxwell-Scott of Abbotsford, Bt. His daughters, Mrs Patricia Maxwell-Scott and Miss Jean Maxwell-Scott, are the present representatives of Sir Walter Scott.

** Renn Dickson Hampden (1793–1868).

Hereford. There was a great furore at Hampden's nomination on account of his supposed unorthodoxy and many, including thirteen bishops, remonstrated; but he proved an excellent prelate and amply justified the confidence of the Prime Minister and his friends.

Early in 1852 Willie Scott learned of the death of his brother Hugh at Draycott House, his Derbyshire home. But his sorrow at the news must have been tempered by further information from the same quarter. Hugh and Sarah Scott were childless, and Hugh had left the whole of the Draycott Estates to his nephew, William Hugh. So the thirty-year-old youngest son of Willie and Susan could forget such unpleasant subjects as Master Attendants and Postmasters, and could return home to become a landed proprietor with ample means to support his new position. He wasted no time in taking over his property; and he very shortly afterwards married Sarah, daughter of Alfred Fellows, a nearby Midlands landowner, and he and his wife settled down to a contented country life at his Derbyshire estate. They had two sons and two daughters.

Though Lady Polwarth was rather fond of complaining of her health at this time, in fact she remained remarkably active and mobile considering her advanced age, staying with her various children, visiting friends, taking the waters and living the life usual for an elderly lady in the nineteenth century. It was not until the early summer of 1853 that she at last began to fail, not until August that her son Polwarth announced to William Scott the death of his 'good mother'. She had been very weak and only semi-conscious for several days, and she died peacefully on the afternoon of Friday, August 19, 1853.[35]

This was bitter news for Raeburn and for the family at Lessudden. All his life William Scott had relied upon some one to help, to advise and to comfort him. First it was his cousin Walter Scott, later Harriet Polwarth: now in his old age—he was almost eighty-two—they were both gone. There is no denying that he was a poor creature. But at least he recognised what he owed to these two fast friends. Sir Walter had ever been his 'dear Cousin'; and he had on several occasions expressed his views on his kinswoman in glowing terms. 'An acquaintance of forty-one years standing and one of the truest and best of friends—always the same', he had written in 1841: 'one of the great and good', he recorded a few years later: no bad epitaphs for Harriet Polwarth.

Epilogue

WILLIE SCOTT did not long outlast his friend Harriet
Polwarth. He was a complete invalid now, confined
to the house and, at the end, to his bed. He died in April
1855 aged eighty-two after having been married to 'the sweet
Susie' for about half a century. He was succeeded by his
eldest surviving child, Robert, who styled himself Robert
Scott of Raeburn and Lessudden. Some six years after his
father's death and at the age of forty-four he married Louisa,
daughter of William Campbell of Ederline, by whom he had
an only son and four daughters. Robert died in 1897 aged
seventy-nine: his widow survived him for thirty years and
died at the age of ninety-two. Robert and Louisa's son
Walter, who like his father styled himself of Raeburn and
Lessudden, was more fond of Scotland's national drink than
was good for him; yet such was his virility that he did not
succumb to the effects until 1935 when he was sixty-nine. He
never married, so with him ended the line of the lairds of
Raeburn. His four sisters, Matilda Wishart, Susan Horsburgh, Louisa and Violet Georgina Margaret, all remained
single and lived for the normal span. Only Violet died comparatively young: she was about sixty-one when she died in
1931. The first and second sisters, born in the same year,
1863, both lived to be eighty-two. The third survived them
all. Louisa Scott of Raeburn died on August 15, 1968. On a
cold summer's day in drenching rain and high wind her
ashes were laid in the burial place of her ancestors in the
grounds of Lessudden. She had died some two and a half
months short of her hundredth year.

So ended the family of Scott of Raeburn. They had lasted

for approximately three centuries. They were plain country lairds, at first comfortably off, but in later years poor and proud and with an acute sense of their own importance. They passed their days at their ancestral home on the outskirts of St Boswells, where they were content to shoot and fish and hunt, to farm their lands, which became greatly reduced in latter years, and to take part in local affairs in the County of Roxburgh. They were no better and no worse than the other border families of like antiquity. But on the Scotts of Raeburn let the greatest of their kinsmen speak. It is fitting that Sir Walter should have the last word:

> They werena ill in them, sir, and that is aye something; they were just decent bien bodies. Ony poor creature that had face to beg got an awmons and welcome; they that were shamefaced gaed by, and twice as welcome. But they keepit an honest walk before God and man, the Croft-angrys, and as I said before, if they did little good, they did as little ill. They lifted their rents and spent them; called in their kain and eat them; gaed to the kirk of a Sunday, bowed civility if folk took aff their bonnets as they gaed by, and lookit as black as sin at them that keepit them on.

Some Abbreviations used in the Notes

BM = British Museum, London.

Border Papers = *The Border Papers, calendar of letters and papers relating to the affairs of the Borders of England and Scotland preserved in her Majesty's Public Record Office, (1560–1603).* (ed. Bain). 2 Vols. 1894–6.

Burghley Papers = *Collection of State Papers . . . left by William Cecil Lord Burghley . . .* (ed. Haynes and Murdin), 2 Vols.

CSP *Henry VIII* = *Calendar of State Papers Letters and Papers, Foreign and Domestic of the Reign of Henry VIII, 1509–47,* 21 Vols.

DNB = Dictionary of National Biography.

Hamilton Papers = *The Hamilton Papers, letters and papers illustrating the political relations of England and Scotland in the sixteenth century* (ed. Bain).

HMC = Historical Manuscripts Commission.

Keith Scott, *Scott 1118–1923* = Captain Keith Scott of Orchards, *Genealogical and Heraldic History of the Border Family of Scotts.*

Lockhart, *Scott* = John Gibson Lockhart, *Life of Sir Walter Scott* (ed. 1839), 10 Vols.

NLS = National Library of Scotland, Edinburgh.

OED = *Oxford English Dictionary.*

PRO = Public Record Office, London.

Scott Journal = *The Journal of Sir Walter Scott from the original manuscript at Abbotsford.*

Scott, *Letters* = *The Letters of Sir Walter Scott* (ed. Grierson), 12 Vols, 1932–7.

Scott, *Minstrelsy* = Sir Walter Scott, *Minstrelsy of the Scottish Border* (ed. Henderson), 4 Vols.

SRO = Scottish Record Office, Edinburgh.

TLS = Times Literary Supplement.

Reference Notes

CHAPTER ONE

1. Johnston, *Place Names of Scotland* (3rd Ed.), 234.

2. *Kalendar of the Scottish Saints*, 281, 318.

3. Scott-Moncrieff, *The Border Abbeys*, 13.

4. The Privy Council to Hertford, April 10th, 1544. BM Add. MS 32654, f. 80. *Hamilton Papers*, II, No. 207. *CSP Henry VIII*, XIX.i, No. 314, 199–200.

5. Hertford, Lisle and Sadler to Henry VIII, 'Legh, Tuesday 6 May at night.' BM, Add. MS. 32654, f. 173. *Hamilton Papers*, II, No. 232. *CSP Henry VIII*, XIX.i, No. 472, 297–8; and Lisle to Paget 'Scribbled at Leith', May 8. PRO Spanish Calendar, VII, 86; *CSP Henry VIII*, III.i, No. 481, 305–6.

6. Scott, appendix to *The Eve of St John*, Note 1. 'Battle of Ancram Moor'.

7. Raids in Scotland. HMC Salisbury, PC I, 180, *CSP Henry VIII*, XIX.ii, No. 625, 372–5. Also see *Raids in Scotland*. BM Harl. MS 1757, ff. 292–302, *CSP Henry VIII*, XIX.ii, No. 331, 13–16. These give a vivid and terrible picture of the damage done to the borders. Haynes, *Burghley Papers*, 50.

8. Elton, *England under the Tudors*, 196.

9. 'The names of the Fortresses, Abbeys, Frere-houses, Market Townes, Villages, Townes and Places brent, raced and cast down by the Commandment of Therll of Hertforde, the King's Majestie's Lieutenant Generall in the North Partes, in the Invasion into the Realme of Scotland, betwene the 8th of Sept. and the 23rd of the same 1545, the 37th year of the King's Royell Majestie's most prousperous and victorious Reign.' *Burghley Papers*, 52.

10. Layton and Redman to Tunstall (Bishop of Durham), *CSP Henry VIII*, XX.i 119. BM Add. MS 32656, f. 172. *Hamilton Papers*, II, No. 414. For further evidence of the havoc inflicted by the Scots, see *CSP Henry VIII*, XX.i I, Nos. 285 and 286. BM Add. MS 32656, ff. 170, 174 and *Hamilton Papers*, II, Nos. 414, 415.

CHAPTER TWO

1. Sir Ralph Bulmer to Duke of Somerset, January 20, 1548–9. *Hamilton Papers*, II, 626.

2. HMC 12th Rep. App. VIII, 144. The exact date of the document cannot be read.

3. *The Scots of Buccleuch*, I, lxx.

4. Keith Scott in *Scott 1118–1923* records four daughters.

5. Scott to Anna Seward, Edinburgh, June 29, 1802. Scott, *Letters*, I, 145.

6. For the whole story see *Register of the Privy Council of Scotland* X, 667; XI, 20, 98–101.

7. *Waverley*, ch. xviii.

8. *Kinmont Willie*, stanzas xliii to xlvi, Scott, *Minstrelsy*, II, 39-70.

9. Scrope to Burghley and to the Privy Council, April 14, 1596. *Border Papers*, II, 120–1.

10. Scrope to Burghley, March 18, 1595/6. *Border Papers*, II, 114–15.

11. Eure (Evers) to Burghley, June 19, 1596. *Border Papers*, II, 139.

12. *Border Papers*, II, 238.

13. Scott, *Minstrelsy*, IV, 379–83.

14. Keith Scott, *Scott 1118–1923*, states that he died in June, 1631.

CHAPTER THREE

1. NLS MS 3842.

2. Lockhart, *Scott*, I, 84–5.

3. MacDougall, Pettworth, 12 January, 1673 to Walter Scott of Raeburne at Lessudden, Scotland. Quoted from a copy in Raeburn's hand. NLS MS 912, f. 172. R.V.

4. William Scott's Memorandum Book, NLS MS 3842.

5. Girouard, *Lessudden House, St Boswells, Country Life*, May 7, 1959.

6. William Scott's Memorandum Book, NLS MS. 3842.

7. *Marmion*, Introduction to Canto Sixth.

8. Lockhart, *Scott*, I, 3.

9. NLS MS 3842, f. 19. Beardie took to spelling his name with only one t.

10. It is now in NLS MS 2889 ff. 39–46V.

11. Alex. Pringle, The Haining, Selkirkshire, January, 30, 1840 to William Scott of Raeburn, Lessudden Place, St Boswells. NLS MS 2890 ff, 148–51.

12. Unto the Queen's most excellent Majesty [Anne], The

Petition of Mark Pringle. NLS MS 2889 ff. 55–8 V.

13. Alex. Pringle, Yair, November 26, 1840 to William Scott of Raeburn, Lessudden Place, St Boswells. NLS MS 2890, f. 157.

14. William Scott of Raeburn, Lessudden Place, November 21, 1846 to Sir William Scott of Ancram. Raeburn Papers SRO, Box 9.

15. Scott, Abbotsford, Saturday evening [October 1830] to William Scott of Raeburn, Lessudden House. NLS MS 2890, f. 92.

CHAPTER FOUR

1. J. L. Hoppringle of Torsonce, Torsonce, October 20, 1707 to Walter Scott at Makerstoun. NLS MS 3843, f. 7.

2. 'McCarston december 26th 1707. Researved in complete payment of the above written account from Walter Scott in McCarston by me Andrew Mitchelhill'. NLS MS 2889, ff. 41 et seq.

3. Pringle, The Haining, Selkirkshire, January 30, 1840 to Scott, Lessudden Place, St Boswells, NLS MS 2890, f. 148.

4. Sir James Steuart to Earl of Loudoun, Edinburgh, March 20th, 1708. NLS MS 2889, f. 64.

5. Pitcairn, 9 Northumberland Street, Edinburgh, May 28, 1851 to Scott, Lessudden Place, St Boswells Green, MS 2890, f. 191.

6. Pringle, *Records of the Pringles*, 176–7.

7. Sir Patrick Scott, Ancrum, October 14, 1714 to Walter Scott, tutor of Raeburn, at Lessudden. NLS MS 2889, f. 66.

8. NLS MS 2899, f. 210

9. Lockhart, *Scott*, I, 4.

CHAPTER FIVE

1. NLS Ch. 1458.

2. 'Acct. of money paid out by Robt. Scott in Sandiknow att Edr. June first 1747 when Raeburn and he went in to burie Miss Isobell Scott, Raeburn's sister.'

3. William Scott to Mr and Mrs Scott, Lessudden, November 22, 1797.

4. William Scott to Barbara Scott, November 22, 1797.

5. William Scott, Cape of Good Hope, October 15, 1798.

6. William Scott, Cape Town, October 29, 1798 to Robert Scott.

7. William Scott, Cape Town, November 1, 1798 to James Scott.

8. William Scott, *Phenix*, St Helena Bay, November 22, 1798 to Robert Scott.

9. William Scott, n.d. to James Scott, Penang.

10. William Scott, Fort St George, July 8, 1800 to Robert Scott,

Rosebank, Kelso, 'left with Tulloh, Brodie and Connell to be forwarded'.

11. William Scott, Fort St George, July 20, 1800 to Mrs Scott, Lessudden, St Boswells.

12. Walter Scott, Edinburgh, November 16, 1793 to William Scott, Lessudden, care of Mr. David Brown, writer, Melrose. NLS MS 2889, f. 79.

PART II

CHAPTER ONE

1. Walter Scott, Edinburgh, March 19, 1795 to William Scott, Prince of Wales's Island, India. To be forwarded by James Hardy Esq. Lombard Street, London. NLS MS 2889, f. 81.

2. Walter Scott, 10 Castle Street, Edinburgh, February 13, 1799 to William Scott, Old Slaughters Coffee House, St Martin's Lane, London. NLS MS 2889, f. 84. His wife was Margaret Charlotte Carpenter and they married at Carlisle on December 24, 1797. She was the daughter of Jean Charpentier of Lyons and Elie Charlotte Volère, his wife. When Mme Charpentier first came to England with her children Charlotte and Charles some years before the Revolution, she found a warm friend in Lord Downshire who after the death of the mother assumed the guardianship of the children. He had obtained for Charles an appointment in the service of the East India Company in which he had risen to the situation of commercial resident at Salem. There appears to be no evidence whatsoever to support Lockhart's statement that Charpentier invested money in Downshire's estates.

3. James Scott, Penang, April 28, 1799 to William Scott of Lessudden. NLS MS Accession 4894. These letters, recently acquired, are not yet in volumes, so there are no folio numbers.

4. John Scott, ? Hansi, January 20, 1804 to William Scott, C/o Messrs. Downie & Maitland, Calcutta. NLS MS Accession 4894.

5. Walter Scott to George Ellis, June 18th, 1804. Scott, *Letters,* Vol. I, 224.

6. Barbara Scott, Lessudden, February 14, 1805 to William Scott, No. 28 North Norfolk Street, Strand, London. NLS MS Accession 4894.

7. Walter Scott, Edinburgh, February 17, 1805 to William Scott, No. 28 Norfolk Street, Strand. NLS MS 2889, f. 93.

8. For Lockhart's description of Ashiestiel, see *Scott,* II, 162–4.

9. Lockhart, *Scott,* II, 161.

10. Barbara Scott, Lessudden, September 20, 1805 to William Scott, Innerleithen, Peebles. NLS MS Accession 4894.

11. William Scott's Memorandum Book. NLS MS 3842.

12. Walter Scott, Edinburgh, June 1, 1805 to William Scott Junior of Raeburn, Innerleithen, By Peebles. NLS MS 2889, f. 95.

13. Walter Scott, Edinburgh, January 7, 1807 to William Scott, junior of Raeburn, Maxpoffle, By St Boswells Green. NLS MS 2889, f. 97.

14. Scott, *Letters,* II, 234.

15. Lockhart, *Scott,* II, 185–6.

16. Lockhart, *Scott,* III, 198–9.

17. Scott, Ashiestiel, Sunday [1809] to Mrs Walter Scott. Scott, *Letters,* II, 234.

18. Quoted by Grierson. *Letters,* III, 429 n.

19. *Scott Journal,* I, 7.

20. For his correspondence with Lord and Lady Abercorn on the affair, see Scott, *Letters* I, 367–70, 373–4, 378, 381, 384, 396, 399; II, 15, 20; VII, 416.

21. Walter Scott, July 20 [1807] to William Scott, Maxpoffle, By St Boswells. NLS MS 2889, f. 99.

22. Scott, *Letters,* XII, 297.

23. William Scott, Maxpoffle, St Boswells, August 27, 1810 to Walter Scott, Ashiestiel, Selkirk. NLS MS 3879, f. 171.

24. Scott, Edinburgh, Thursday [April 12, 1811] to Charles Erskine, Writer, Melrose. Scott, *Letters,* II, 476.

25. Hugh Scott, London, October 9, 1810 to William Scott, Maxpoffle, St Boswells. NLS MS Accession 4894.

26. Robert Scott, London, May 19, 1812 to William Scott, Crown Inn, Harrogate. NLS MS Accession 4894.

27. Robert Scott, London, May 25, 1812 to William Scott, Crown, Harrogate. NLS MS Accession 4894.

28. Robert Scott, Cheltenham, July 5, 1812 to William Scott, Maxpoffle, St Boswells. NLS MS Accession 4894.

29. Robert Scott, Lessudden. July 27, 1812 to William Scott, Maxpoffle, Kelso. NLS MS Accession 4894.

30. Robert Scott, Lessudden, July 28, 1812 to William Scott, Maxpoffle, Kelso. NLS MS Accession 4894

31. Walter Scott, Edinburgh, February 3 [1811] to William Scott, Maxpoffle, By St Boswells. NLS MS 2889, f. 103.

32. William Scott, Maxpoffle, February 19, 1811 to Walter Scott, North Castle Street, Edinburgh. NLS MS 3880, f. 49.

33. William Scott, Maxpoffle, January 18, 1812 to Walter Scott, North Castle Street, Edinburgh. NLS MS 3882, f. 32.

34. Walter Scott, Edinburgh, January 28th, 1812 to William Scott of Maxpoffle, NLS MS 2889, f. 105.

35. *Scott Journal,* I, 90.

36. 'Maxpopple came with us as far as Lessudden, and we stopped and made a pilgrimage to Fair Maiden Lilliard's Stone, which has been restored lately to the credit of Mr Walker of Muirhouselaw.' *Scott Journal* I, 388. Maiden Lilliard was a Border amazon slain at Ancrum Moor, 1545.

37. Scott, Abbotsford, November 3, 1812 to Christian Rutherford. Scott, *Letters*, III, 192.

38. William Scott, Maxpoffle, February 4, 1812 to Walter Scott. NLS MS 2889, f. 107.

39. Scott, Castle Street, November 17, 1813 to Duke of Buccleuch. Scott. *Letters*, III, 383.

40. Duke of Buccleuch to Scott. NLS MS 3882, f. 49.

41. Walter Scott, Abbotsford, to Robert Southey, Keswick, September 1, 1813. Scott, *Letters*, III, 335–6.

42. Scott, Abbotsford, August 24, 1813 to Duke of Buccleuch. Scott, *Letters*, III, 324.

43. Duke of Buccleuch, Drumlanrig Castle, to Walter Scott, August 28, 1813. NLS MS 3884, f. 236.

44. Scott, Abbotsford, September 3, 1813 to Duke of Buccleuch. Scott has dated letter September 3rd, but 5th seems more likely. Scott, *Letters*, III, 346–7.

45. Hugh Scott of Harden to Walter Scott, Castle Street, Edinburgh. NLS MS 3885, f. 46.

46. Scott, Abbotsford, September 5 [1813] to Mrs Walter Scott at Mrs Scott of Raeburn's, Lessudden, St Boswells. Scott, *Letters*, III, 353–4.

47. Robert Scott, Somerset Coffee House, Strand, December 28 [18]13 to William Scott, Maxpoffle, St Boswells Green. NLS MS Accession 4894.

48. William Lindsay, Feddinch, January 7, 1814 to William Scott, Maxpoffle, St Boswells. NLS MS Accession 4894.

49. Robert Scott, Somerset Coffee House, Strand, January 7 and 20, 1814 to William Scott, Maxpoffle, St Boswells. NLS MS Accession 4894.

50. William Scott to Walter Scott, May 28, 1814. NLS MS 2889, f. 113.

51. Hugh Scott, London, September 8, 1814 to William Scott of Maxpoffle, St Boswells. NLS MS Accession 4894.

52. Robert Scott, Penang, October 15, 1814 to William Scott, Maxpoffle, St Boswells Green. NLS MS Accession 4894.

53. William Scott, Maxpoffle, September 11, 1817 to Walter Scott. NLS MS 2889, f. 143.

54. Walter Scott to William Scott, Tuesday Maxpoffle. St Boswells, n.d. [September 9, 1817]. NLS MS 2889, f. 141.

F*

55. Scott, Abbotsford, September 20 [1817] to Duke of Buccleuch. Scott, *Letters,* IV, 513–14.

56. Duke of Buccleuch, Drumlg. Castle, September 27, 1817 to Walter Scott, Abbotsford, Melrose. NLS MS 3888, f. 181. Partly quoted by Scott to his cousin, October 5, 1817. NLS MS 2889, f. 144.

57. Walter Scott, Abbotsford, Edinburgh, November 24, 1817 to William Scott. NLS MS 2889, ff. 144.

58. Walter Scott, Abbotsford, Friday night [January 2, 1818] to William Scott, Maxpoffle, St Boswells. NLS MS 2889, f. 152.

CHAPTER TWO

1. Walter Scott, Edinburgh, January 28 [1819] to William Scott younger of Raeburn, Maxpoffle, St Boswells Green. NLS MS 3889, f. 165.

2. Sir Walter Blunt, I King Henry IV, V, iii.

3. Walter Scott, Edinburgh, December 7, 1818 to Morritt, M. P., Rokeby. Scott, *Letters,* V, 260–1.

4. See article by Professor A. Aspinall, *Walter Scott's Baronetcy, some new letters,* in TLS October 25, 1947. I am grateful to Dr J. C. Corson for having brought this to my notice.

5. Duke of Buccleuch, Bowhill, December 8, 1818 to Walter Scott, Castle Street, Edinburgh. NLS MS 3889, f. 273.

6. Walter Scott to William Scott, Edinburgh, January 28 [1819]. NLS MS 3889, f. 165.

7. Walter Scott, Edinburgh, February 3 [1819] to William Scott, Maxpoffle, St Boswells. NLS MS 3889, f. 167.

8. William Lindsay, Feddinch, May 25, 1819 to William Scott of Maxpoffle, St Boswells. NLS MS Accession 4894.

9. Sir Walter Scott, Edinburgh, June 10, 1819 to William Scott of Maxpoffle, St Boswells Green. NLS MS 3889, f. 175.

10. Scott, Edinburgh April 13 [1821] to Lord Montagu. Scott, *Letters,* VI, 411–12.

11. Scott, Edinburgh April 15 [1821] to Lord Montagu. Scott, *Letters,* VI, 413–14.

12. Sir Walter Scott, Edinburgh, April 11 [1821] to William Scott. NLS MS 2889, f. 179.

13. Note by Mr George A. M. Wood. *Notes and Queries,* ccix, 471.

14. *Scott Journal,* II, 122.

15. Sir Walter Scott,n. d. [April 29, 1821] to William Scott yr. of Raeburn. NLS MS 2889, f. 181.

16. Sir Walter Scott to William Scott n.d. [April, May? 1821]. NLS MS 2889, f. 189.

17. Sir Walter Scott, Abbotsford, Wednesday [April 1821]. NLS MS 2889, f. 185.

18. *Hamlet,* III, ii. Sir Walter Scott, May 1 [1821], Abbotsford to Lord Montagu. Scott, *Letters,* VI, 428–30.

19. John Rutherford, Edgerston, May 5, 1821 to Sir Walter Scott, Abbotsford, Melrose. NLS MS 3892, f. 123.

20. Sir Walter Scott, Edinburgh, May 18, 1821 to William Scott, Maxpoffle, St Boswells. NLS MS 2889, f. 190.

21. Scott, Abbotsford, April 13 [1826] to Montagu, Ditton Park. Scott, *Letters,* IX, 502.

22. John Richardson, 5 Fludyer Street, Westminster, May 21, 1821 to Sir Walter Scott. NLS MS 2889, f. 193.

23. Scott, Edinburgh May 15, [1821] to Lothian. *Notes and Queries,* ccix, 469–71.

24. Scott, Edinburgh, May 18, 1821 to William Scott. NLS MS 2889, f. 190.

25. Lothian, London, May 22 [1821] to Scott, *Notes and Queries,* ccix, 472. NLS MS 3892, f. 134.

26. Sir Walter Scott, May 24 [1821] to William Scott, Maxpoffle, St Boswells. NLS MS 2889, f. 193.

27. Sir Walter Scott, Edinburgh, May 30 [1821] to Lord Montagu, 24 Portland Place [London]. Scott, *Letters,* VI, 455–6.

28. Sir Walter Scott, Blair Adam, June 11, 1821 to Lord Montagu. Scott, *Letters,* VI, 460.

29. Lord Montagu, Thomas's Hotel, June 13 1821. NLS MS 3892, ff. 165 et seq.

30. Sir Walter Scott, June 16, 1821 to Lord Montagu. Scott, *Letters,* VI, 475–6.

31. Lord Montagu, Bothwell Castle, September 1 [1821] to Sir Walter Scott. NLS MS 3893, f. 62.

32. Sir Walter Scott, Abbotsford, September 8 [1821] to Lord Montagu, Drumlanrig Castle. Scott, *Letters,* VII, 9–10.

33. Sir Walter Scott, Edinburgh, July 3, 1821 to William Scott, Maxpoffle, St Boswells. NLS MS 2889, f. 196.

34. Sir Walter Scott, Edinburgh, February 10 [1822] to William Scott younger of Raeburn, Maxpoffle, by St Boswells. NLS MS 2889, f. 203.

35. Sir Walter Scott, Edinburgh, February 24 [1822] to William Scott, Maxpoffle, St Boswells. NLS MS 2889, f. 207.

36. Rutherford and Scott, Jedburgh, April 21, 1822 to Montagu. Scott, *Letters,* VII, 131–2.

37. Scott, Abbotsford, April 28 [1822] to Montagu, Ditton Park, Windsor. Scott, *Letters,* VII, 148.

38. Scott, Abbotsford, May 15 [1822] a Monsr. Walter Scott

Lieutenant Dans Le 15me Regiment Des Houssards de Sa Majesté Britannique a Berlin. Scott, *Letters*, VII, 165.

39. Scott, Abbotsford, October 6 [1822] to Hugh Scott, Draycott Manor, Near Derby. Scott, *Letters*, VII, 262.

40. Scott, Abbotsford, October 7 [1822] to Lieutenant Walter Scott, 15th Hussars, at Dresden. In fact Walter was on half pay at this time. He merely happened to be at Dresden during his travels. Scott, *Letters*, VII, 264.

CHAPTER THREE

1. Sir Walter Scott, Edinburgh, February 5 [1824] to William Scott, Maxpoffle, St Boswells. NLS MS 2890, f. 18.

2. Sir Walter Scott, Castle Street, Thusday [February 12 1824] to William Scott younger of Raeburn, Maxpoffle, St Boswells. NLS MS 2890, f. 17.

3. Sir Walter Scott, Abbotsford, Sunday [April 4 1824] to William Scott, Maxpoffle, St Boswells. NLS MS 2890, f. 23.

4. Sir Walter Scott, Edinburgh, May 25 [1824] to William Scott. NLS MS 2890, f. 27.

5. Sir Walter Scott, Abbotsford, September 30 [1824] to William Scott, Maxpoffle, St Boswells. NLS MS 2890, f. 35.

6. Captain Basil Hall's Journal, 'Abbotsford, January 7th, 1825'.

7. Sir Walter Scott, Edinburgh, January 21 [1825] to William Scott younger of Raeburn, Maxpoffle, St Boswells. NLS MS 2890, f. 41.

8. Scott, Edinburgh, January 28 [1825] to Montagu. Scott, *Letters*, VIII, 503–4.

9. As from January 30th,—Scott—Abbotsford, May 1, 1825 to William Scott [Younger] of Raeburn. Scott, *Letters*, IX, 100.

10. Scott, Edinburgh, January 31 [P.M. 1825] to Montagu, Ditton Park, Windsor. Scott, *Letters*, VIII, 506.

11. Scott, Edinburgh, March 5 [1825] to Hugh Scott, Draycott, near Derby. Scott, *Letters*, IX, 20.

12. Scott, n.d. [P.M. February 18, 1825] to Montagu, Ditton, Windsor. Scott, *Letters*, IX, 6–7.

13. William Scott, Maxpoffle, January 31, 1825 to Scott. NLS MS 2890, f. 43.

14. Sir Walter Scott, Edinburgh, Wednesday [June 1825] to William Scott, Maxpoffle. NLS MS 2890, f. 55.

15. Scott, n.d. [May 10, 11, 1825] to Lord Montagu. Scott, *Letters*, IX, 110.

16. William Scott, Shaw Wood, January 16, 1826 to Sir Walter Scott, North Castle Street, Edinburgh. NLS MS 3902, f. 17.

17. William Scott, Shaw Wood, February 20, 1826 to Sir Walter Scott. NLS MS 3902, f. 77.

18. Robert Scott, Penang, August 13, 1825 to William Scott, Maxpoffle. NLS MS Accession 4894.

19. Robert Scott, Penang, January 5, 1826 to William Scott, Maxpoffle. NLS MS Accession 4894.

20. Robert Scott, Penang, October 23, 1826 to William Scott, Shaw Cottage, Near Shaw, Selkirk. NLS MS Accession 4894.

21. *Scott Journal*, I, 187.

22. Scott, Monday May 15 [P.M. 1826] to Charles Scott, at Brazen Nose College, Oxford. Scott, *Letters*, X, 36.

23. *Scott Journal*, I, 188. See also I, 180.

24. Scott, Edinburgh, December 9 [1826] to Croker. Scott. *Letters*, X, 137–8.

25. *Guy Mannering*, Chapter II.

26. *Guy Mannering*, Chapter V.

27. Scott, Abbotsford, July 15 [1828] to Lockhart. Scott, *Letters*, X, 471.

28. *Scott Journal*, July 21, 1826.

29. Sir Walter Scott, Abbotsford, October 22, 1828 to William Scott junior of Raeburn. Endorsed on the death of my worthy Mother. NLS MS 2890, f. 76.

30. Sir Walter Scott, Abbotsford, October 24 [1828] to Mrs Lockhart, Brighton. Scott, *Letters*, XI, 22.

31. Robert Scott, Penang, May 18, 1829 to William Scott, Maxpoffle, Near St Boswells Green. NLS MS Accession 4894.

32. Lockhart, *Scott*, VI, 85.

33. *Scott Journal*, II, 272.

34. Smout, *A History of the Scottish People, 1560–1830*, 504.

35. Lockhart, *Scott*, IV, 276–7.

36. *Scott Journal*, April 25, 1829, II, 274–5.

37. Sir Walter Scott, Edinburgh, Wednesday [May 19, 1830] to William Scott of Raeburn, Maxpoffle, St Boswells. NLS MS 2890, f. 84.

38. *Scott Journal*, May 23, 1830, II, 325–6.

39. Robert Scott, Penang, June 2 and 12, 1830 to William Scott, Shaw Cottage, Nr. Selkirk. NLS MS Accession 4894.

40. Robert Scott, Draycott, Near Derby, July 6, 1830 to William Scott, Lessudden House, St Boswells Green. NLS MS Accession 4894.

41. *Scott Journal*, July 16 and 17, 1830.

42. Robert Scott, Salutation Inn, Perth, September 2, 1830 to William Scott, Lessudden House, St Boswells Green. NLS MS Accession 4894.

43. Robert Scott, Mackenzie's Hotel, Edinburgh, September 9, 1830 to William Scott, Lessudden House, St Boswells Green. NLS MS Accession 4894.

44. Charles Scott, Penang October 5, 1830 to William Scott, Maxpoffle, Nr. St Boswells Green and Robert Scott, Edinburgh, October 25, 1830 to William Scott of Raeburn, Selkirk. NLS MS Accession 4894.

45. William Scott, Lessudden Place, October 25, 1830 to Robert Scott (from a copy in Raeburn's hand). NLS MS Accession 4894.

46. Robert Scott, Edinburgh, October 21, 1830 to William Scott, Lessudden House, St Boswells Green. NLS MS Accession 4894.

47. Robert Scott, Edinburgh, January 22, 1830 [*sic* but error for 1831] to William Scott of Raeburn, Selkirk. NLS MS Accession 4894.

48. Alexander Scott, Edinburgh, Tuesday night March 8, 1831 to William Scott of Raeburn, St Boswells Green. NLS MS Accession 4894.

49. Robert Scott, Edinburgh, March 14, 1831 to William Scott of Raeburn, St Boswells, NLS MS Accession 4894.

50. Alexander Scott, Edinburgh, May 14, 1831 to William Scott of Raeburn, St Boswells Green. NLS MS Accession 4894.

51. *Scott Journal*, II, 395.

52. Alexander Scott, Edinburgh, November 10, 1831 to William Scott of Raeburn, St Boswells Green. NLS MS Accession 4894.

53. Robert Scott, Edinburgh, November 11, 1831 to William Scott of Raeburn, Lessudden House, by St Boswells Green. NLS MS Accession 4894.

54. Alexander Scott, Edinburgh, November 23, 1831 to William Scott of Raeburn, Selkirk. NLS MS Accession 4894.

55. His sister, Susan Elizabeth, Willie and Susan Scott's third daughter.

56. Alexander Scott, Edinburgh, December 11, 1831 to William Scott, Sheriff-Substitute, Selkirk. NLS MS Accession 4894.

57. Alexander Scott, Edinburgh, December 27, 1831 to William Scott of Raeburn, Selkirk. NLS MS Accession 4894.

58. Robert Scott, Edinburgh, January 24, 1832 to William Scott of Raeburn, Selkirk. NLS MS Accession 4894.

59. Robert Scott, Edinburgh, April 14, 1832 to William Scott of Raeburn, Lessudden House, St Boswells Green. NLS MS Accession 4894.

60. Alexander Scott, Edinburgh, May 1, 1831 [*sic*, mistake for 1832] to William Scott of Raeburn, Selkirk. NLS MS Accession 4894.

61. Alexander Scott, Edinburgh, June 6, 1832 to William Scott of Raeburn, Lessudden Place. NLS MS Accession 4894.

62. Alexander Scott, Edinburgh, June 26, 1832 to William Scott of Raeburn, Lessudden Place. NLS MS Accession 4894.

63. William Scott, n.d. [1826] to Sir Walter Scott. NLS MS 3903, f. 248.

64. William Scott, Selkirk, December 25, 1830 to Sir Walter Scott of Abbotsford, Melrose. NLS MS 3915, f. 196.

65. William Scott, Selkirk, May 25, 1831 to Sir Walter Scott of Abbotsford, Melrose. NLS MS 3918, f. 71.

66. Chisholm, *Sir Walter Scott as a Judge,* 90

67. Walter Scott, St James's Hotel, Jermyn Street, Monday 3 p.m. [July 2, 1832] to William Scott. NLS MS 2890, f. 112.

68. John Gibson Lockhart, Abbotsford, July 12, 1832 to William Scott. NLS MS 2890, f. 115.

69. John Gibson Lockhart, Abbotsford, Monday evening, July 30, 1832 to William Scott of Raeburn, Lessudden, St Boswells Green. NLS MS 2890, f. 117.

70. Lockhart, *Scott,* VII, 394.

CHAPTER FOUR

1. Alexander Scott, Edinburgh. August 7, 1832 to William Scott of Raeburn, Selkirk. NLS MS Accession 4894.

2. D. Cleghorn, Edinburgh, October 8, 1832 to William Scott of Raeburn, Lessudden House by St Boswells Green. NLS MS Accession 4894.

3. Robert Scott, Edinburgh, October 13, 1832 to William Scott, Lessudden House, St Boswells Green. NLS MS Accession 4894.

4. William Scott, January 3, 1833 to Robert Scott (from a copy in William's hand). NLS MS Accession 4894.

5. Robert Scott, Edinburgh, February 12, 1832 to William Scott of Raeburn, Lessudden House. NLS MS Accession 4894.

6. Robert Scott, Edinburgh, March 19, 1823 to William Scott of Raeburn Lessudden House, St Boswells Green. NLS MS Accession 4894.

7. Robert Scott, Edinburgh, May 15, 1833 to William Scott of Raeburn, Lessudden House, St Boswells NLS MS Accession 4894.

8. Alexander Scott, Draycott, May 25, 1833 to William Scott, Lessudden Place, St Boswells, Roxburghshire. NLS MS Accession 4894.

9. Alexander Scott, London, 15 Broad Street Buildings, Monday June 3, 1833 to William Scott, Lessudden House, St Boswells Green, Roxburgh, Scotland. NLS MS Accession 4894.

10. James Metcalfe, Steward to the Duke of Buccleuch.

11. William Scott, June 20, 1832 to Alexander Scott, Mrs Bothwell, 15 Broad Street Buildings, London. NLS MS Accession 4894.

12. Alexander Scott, London, 15 Broad Street Buildings, June 27, 1832 to William Scott, St Boswells Green. NLS MS Accession 4894.

13. Alexander Scott, London, 15 Broad Street Buildings, July 2, 1833 to William Scott, St Boswells Green, Roxburghshire. NLS MS Accession 4894.

14. Robert Scott, Edinburgh, September 20, 1833 to William Scott of Raeburn, Lessudden House, St Boswells Green. NLS MS Accession 4894.

15. Rowland Hill, first Viscount Hill. (1772–1842) General.

16. Alexander Scott, London, 24 Cecil Street, Strand, Saturday, October 11, 1833 to William Scott, St Boswells Green, N.B. NLS MS Accession 4894.

17. Alexander Scott, Paris, No. 15 Quai Malaquae, Sunday October 20, 1833 to William Scott, St Boswells. NLS MS Accession 4894.

18. Robert Scott, Hastings, Sussex, October 21, 1833 to William Scott, Lessudden House, St Boswells Green. NLS MS Accession 4894.

19. Robert Scott, 8 Pelham Crescent, Hastings, November 13, 1833 to William Scott, Lessudden House, St Boswells Green, Roxburghshire. NLS MS Accession 4894.

20. Alexander Scott, Paris, Rue Fanby St. Honoré, December 6, 1833 to William Scott, St Boswells Green, Roxburghshire, Scotland. NLS MS Accession 4894.

21. Robert Scott, Hastings, February 11, 1834 to William Scott of Raeburn, 1 Annandale Street, Edinburgh. NLS MS Accession 4894.

22. Robert Scott, Hastings, March 11, 1834 to William Scott of Raeburn, Lessudden House, St Boswells Green, Roxburghshire. NLS MS Accession 4894.

23. Alexander Scott, Hastings, April 18, 1834 to William Scott, Lessudden Place, St Boswells Green, Roxburgh. N.B. NLS MS Accession 4894.

24. Alexander Scott, Hastings, Sunday May 3, 1834 to William Scott, Lessudden Place, St Boswells Green, Roxburghshire. NLS MS Accession 4894.

25. Alexander Scott, London, May 16, 1834 to William Scott, Lessudden Place, St Boswells Green, Roxburghshire. N.B. NLS MS Accession 4894.

26. Alexander Scott, London, May 27, 1834, 18 Cecil Street,

Strand to William Scott of Raeburn, St Boswells Green, Roxburgh-shire, N.B. NLS MS Accession 4894.

27. Robert Scott, Tunbridge Wells, May 23, 1834 to William Scott of Raeburn, Lessudden House, St Boswells Green, Roxburgh, N.B. NLS MS Accession 4894.

28. Alexander Scott, No. 1 Somerset Place, Friday June 6, 1834 to William Scott, Lessudden Place, St Boswells Green, Roxburgh, N.B. NLS MS Accession 4894.

29. Alexander Scott, London, 18 Cecil Street, Monday June 16, 1834 to William Scott of Raeburn, Moffat, Dumfriesshire, N.B. NLS MS Accession 4894.

30. Robert Scott, Tunbridge Wells, June 24, 1834 to William Scott of Raeburn, Lessudden House, St Boswells Green, Roxburgh-shire, N.B. NLS MS Accession 4894.

31. Robert Scott, 5 Putney Terrace, September 4, 1834 to William Scott, Lessudden House, St Boswells Green, Roxburgh-shire, N.B. NLS MS Accession 4894.

32. Robert Scott, Fanchel, Madeira, November 18, 1834 to William Scott, Lessudden House, St Boswells Green, Roxburghshire, N.B. NLS MS Accession 4894.

33. Alexander Scott, Penang, November 24, 1834 to William Scott, St Boswells Green, Roxburghshire, Scotland, NLS. MS Accession 4894.

34. Robert Scott, Fanchel, Madeira, June 13, 1835 to William Scott, Lessudden House, St Boswells Green, Roxburgh, N.B. NLS MS Accession 4894.

35. Robert Scott, Fanchel, Madeira, August 20, 1835, to William Scott, Lessudden House, St Boswells Green, Roxburgh, N.B. NLS MS Accession 4894.

36. Robert Scott, Madeira, July 8, 1836 to Violet Scott, Lessudden House, St Boswells Green, Roxburghshire, N.B. Endorsed in William Scott's hand 'Last letter from Robert Scott'. NLS MS Accession 4894.

37. Barbara Scott, Berness Street, Berness Hotel, September 10, 1836 to William Scott of Raeburn, Lessudden Place, St Boswells Green, Roxburghshire. Endorsed 'From London: Death of our beloved brother Robert.' NLS MS Accession 4894.

38. Alexander Scott, Penang, March, 1837, to William Scott, St Boswells Green, Roxburgh, Scotland. NLS MS Accession 4894.

CHAPTER FIVE

1. Walter Scott, Abbotsford, January 2, 1817 to Duke of Bucc-leuch, Scott, *Letters* IV, 349–50.

'Let that be wrought which Mat doth say:
Yea, quoth the Erle, but not today.'

Prior, *Erl Roberts' Mice: In Chaucer's Style.*

2. Gualterus Scott, Rosebank, August 23, 1795 to Clerk. Scott, *Letters,* I, 269.

3. Lockhart, *Scott,* I, 285–6.

4. Lady Polwarth, Mertoun, February 1840, to William Scott of Raeburne [*sic*], Lessudden Place, Raeburne Papers, SRO Box 8.

5. Lady Polwarth, Wednesday (*c.* March 1845) to William Scott. Raeburn Papers, SRO Box 9.

6. Lady Polwarth, Thursday n.d. [1840] to William Scott. Raeburn Papers, SRO Box 9. Lady Louisa was the authoress of the introductory anecdotes prefixed to Lord Warncliffe's edition of *The Letters and Works of Lady Mary Wortley Montagu* (1837). She died unmarried in August, 1851, aged 94.

7. Lady Polwarth, n.d. [1841] to William Scott. Raeburn Papers, SRO Box 9.

8. Lady Polwarth n.d. [December 1841] to William Scott. Raeburn Papers, SRO Box 9.

9. Lady Polwarth September 10, 1841 to William Scott of Raeburn. Raeburn Papers, SRO Box 9.

10. Lady Polwarth, Thursday [March 1838] to William Scott of Raeburn, Lessudden Place. Raeburn Papers, SRO Box 9.

11. Alexander Scott, Penang, April 29, 1837 to William Scott. St Boswells Green, Roxburghshire, Scotland. NLS MS Accession 4894.

12. William Scott, Lessudden Place, St Boswells, Roxburghshire, May 12, 1828 [*sic* mistake for 1838] to His Grace the Duke of Wellington. (Taken from a copy in William Scott's hand), Raeburn Papers, SRO Box 8.

13. Duke of Wellington, London, May 17, 1838 to William Scott, Lessudden Place, St Boswells, Roxburghshire. NLS MS 3843.

14. Alexander Scott, Penang, September 4, 1838 to William Scott, Lessudden Place, St Boswells Green, Roxburghshire, N.B. NLS MS Accession 4854.

15. William Scott, Singapore, November 17, 1838 to William Scott, Lessudden Place by St Boswells Green, Roxburghshire, N.B. NLS MS Accession 4854.

16. Lady Polwarth, Thursday [October 1840] to William Scott of Raeburn. Raeburn Papers, SRO Box 8.

17. William Scott of Raeburn, Ln. Pl. October 21, 1840 to Lady Polwarth (from a copy in William Scott's hand,) Raeburn Papers, SRO Box 8.

18. Lady Polwarth, Sunday night March 7 [1841] to William Scott of Raeburn, Lessudden Place. Raeburn Papers, SRO Box 9.

19. Lady Polwarth, Friday July 23 [1841] to Mrs Scott of Raeburn. Raeburn Papers, SRO Box 9.

20. Anne Scott had married in December 1831 Charles Baillie, (1804–79) a rising Scottish lawyer one day to be a judge with the title of Lord Jerviswoode.

21. Lady Polwarth, Wednesday night [August 25, 1841] to William Scott. Raeburn Papers, SRO Box 9.

22. Lady Polwarth, n.d. [1841] to William Scott. Raeburn Papers, SRO Box 9.

23. Lady Polwarth, Brighton, February 21, 1843 to William Scott of Raeburn, Lessudden Place, St Boswells, Roxburghshire. Raeburn Papers, SRO Box 9. Her son-in-law Colonel Charles Wyndham, was an MP at this time.

24. Lady Polwarth, Rogate, May 10 [1842] to William Scott of Raeburn, Lessudden House. Raeburn Papers, SRO Box 9.

25. Lord Polwarth, Mertoun House, December 30, 1842 to William Scott of Raeburn. Raeburn Papers SRO Box 9.

26. Lady Polwarth, 28 Charles Street, Grosvenor Place, London, May 7, 1843 to William Scott of Raeburn, Lessudden Place, St Boswells, Roxburghshire. Raeburn Papers, SRO Box 9.

27. Lord Polwarth, Mertoun, May 21, 1843 to William Scott. Raeburn Papers, SRO Box 9.

28. Lady Polwarth, 5 Lewes Crescent, Brighton [October 18], 1843, to William Scott of Raeburn, Lessudden Place, St Boswells, Roxburghshire. Raeburn Papers, SRO Box 9.

29. Lady Polwarth, Rogate, January 6, 1845 to William Scott of Raeburn, Lessudden Place, St Boswells, Roxburghshire. Raeburn Papers, SRO Box 9.

30. Lord Polwarth, Mertoun House, November 15, 1845 to William Scott. Raeburn Papers, SRO Box 9.

31. Lord Polwarth, n.d. to William Scott of Raeburn, Lessudden Place. Raeburn Papers, SRO Box 9.

32. Lord Polwarth, Mertoun, January 7, 1846 to William Scott. Raeburn Papers, SRO Box 9.

33. Church, Singapore, June 7, 1847 to William Hugh Scott. NLS MS Accession 4894.

34. Church, Singapore, June 15, 1847 to William Hugh Scott, NLS MS Accession 4894.

35. Lord Polwarth, Mertoun, August 22, 1853 to William Scott. Raeburn Papers, SRO Box 10.

Index